Many Books, Many Stories

This book is part of Peter Lang Education list.
Every volume is peer reviewed and meets
the highest quality standards for content and production.

PETER LANG
New York • Berlin • Brussels • Lausanne • Oxford

Many Books, Many Stories

Using Children's and Young Adult Literature to Open Classroom Conversations

Edited by
Kathleen Olmstead and Serena Troiani

PETER LANG
New York • Berlin • Brussels • Lausanne • Oxford

Library of Congress Cataloging-in-Publication Control Number: 2022042045

Bibliographic information published by **Die Deutsche Nationalbibliothek**.
Die Deutsche Nationalbibliothek lists this publication in the "Deutsche
Nationalbibliografie"; detailed bibliographic data are available
on the Internet at http://dnb.d-nb.de/.

ISBN 978-1-4331-9913-4 (hardcover)
ISBN 978-1-4331-9914-1 (paperback)
ISBN 978-1-4331-9915-8 (ebook pdf)
ISBN 978-1-4331-9916-5 (epub)
DOI 10.3726/b20112

© 2023 Peter Lang Publishing, Inc., New York
80 Broad Street, 5th floor, New York, NY 10004
www.peterlang.com

We dedicate this collection to our students ~ with many thanks for their stories that have been shared— and for the stories that have yet to be told.

Table of Contents

Foreword

BOBBIE KABUTO

Many Books, Many Stories: Using Children's and Young Adult Literature to Open Classroom Conversations should have a special place on every teacher's bookshelf. As I read through the chapters, I recognized how concepts, such as mirrors and windows, multiculturalism, antiracist pedagogy, narratives and counter narratives, created a variety of complementary storylines on the importance of using quality children's and young adult literature in today's classroom. Through these storylines, the chapters came together in powerful ways to challenge deficit-oriented views of diversity through literature in its most general sense: multicultural literature, global literature, children's literature, young adult literature, and multimodal literature. Together the chapters tackle two overarching questions: *What is diversity?* and *Why is it important to address diversity through literature?*

What is Diversity?

As Section 2 of this volume illustrates, a definition of diversity is difficult to capture. A general and modest definition of diversity refers to the dynamic states of being different or having elements or varieties that are distinct (Arce-Trigatti & Anderson, 2018; Faist, 2010). In Chapter 3, Kelly, Tirrito, and Troiani discuss gender diversity and how they led a school-wide book club to address the changing and growing diversity of the local community. Ashton, Flugel, and Kelly in Chapter 4 explore stereotypes and the objectification of disability in relation to notions of ableism. Shema in Chapter 5 discussed how a single profile of what it means to be a family does not reflect the real-life and cultural ways that family is defined.

A closer read through the chapters, however, suggest a more sophisticated definition of diversity is needed in order to address the pluralism and complexity within diversity. It is that complexity that impacts how we see and interact with the world and how the world, and individuals within it, see and interact with us (Faist, 2010; Nieto, 2015). The complexity within diversity reflects the concept of pluralism to suggest that there is no single group of diverse people (i.e. all Blacks are African Americans), but rather there are multiple layers of diversity that can intersect, complement, and challenge other layers (Faist, 2010). Through this definition, the collection of chapters in this volume challenge the notion that diversity can be seen as some type of decoration, as often portrayed in some multicultural curricular units to books (Botelho & Rudman, 2009).

A more nuanced definition of diversity, rather, is viewed as a set of practices composed of intersectional self-identities (DiAngelo, 2011; Oluo, 2019). Ashton, et al. (Chapter 4), Harrison and Spinelli (Chapter 6), and Boehm and Worlds (Chapter 7) used the term intersectionality coined by Crenshaw (1991) "to denote the various ways in which race and gender interact to share the multiple dimensions of Black women's employment experiences" (p. 1244). As the authors show, intersectionality is necessary to understand how educators can use literature and pedagogy to disrupt deficit-oriented narratives to diversity. Ashton, Flugel, and Kelly, for instance, poignantly argue that the majority of research on disability, through the framework of Disability Studies, has been "dominated by White voices and experiences" (this volume). Furthermore, they contend that the current literature that addresses disabilities provides problematic stereotypes and ignores the voices of individuals of color. The authors write, "Disability is an identity that one can have alongside many identities including, but not limited to, race, gender, class, ethnicity, sexuality, and religion (Beverley, 2009; Thomson, 1997)."

I add that black and brown students are disportionality overrepresented in disability categories and more associated with being "at risk of failure" (Noguera, 2016). There is a structural inequality built into the system that examines 'ability' through normative assessments practices that do little to consider socioeconomic class, educational histories, race, and language backgrounds of students who we educate.

Through the lens of intersectionality, the authors in this volume ask the tough question: Whose voices are being silenced and whose voices are being heard in K-12 classrooms through literature? To address this question, Olmstead, Colantonio-Yurko, and Hutchings (Chapter 1), Paugh and Acevedo-Aquino (Chapter 2) and Kelly, Tirrito, and Troiani (Chapter 3) explore notions of "mirror texts." They use the term to describe how readers can see themselves represented within text, illustrations, or combination of the two. The authors argue that it is also through mirror text that we recognize whose voices exist on the fringes of the diversity work and how teachers can move those voices from the fringes to the center of curriculum and pedagogy.

I, for instance, identify as an Asian American (a person of brown color) cisgender individual. Approaching 50 years old and having lived almost a half a century has been a blessing. I never really thought about my age until recently when I began reflecting on how much has changed and, unfortunately, not changed in the world. When I was in elementary school, the landscape of children's literature looked quite different than it does today (Larrick, 1965). When I reflect on the children's book that could pose as a mirror text for me as a child, I am at a loss. At the time, the picturebook in probably the majority of K-2 classrooms that featured Asian characters was the *Five Chinese Brothers* (Bishop, 1996), a folktale of five brothers who have a special power. The older brother is accused of murder and the brothers use their powers when they are being punished for the proposed crime. At the end of the story, none of the brothers are punished and return to their home to live with their mother. More disturbing are the pictures that show each brother smiling as they are awaiting their punishment. The book, which was written and illustrated by a white author and illustrator in 1938 and reissued in 1965, was read aloud by my first grade teacher and is now banned by many school districts for its representation of Asians and violence.

This book did little to act as a healthy mirror text. In some ways, I was forced to see some of myself in the text by having the teacher read it aloud and by my classmates asking if I dress like the brothers at home. The book did not represent the ways that I self-identified as an Asian American. I have loving parents and grew up in a single parent household for part of my childhood to an Asian mother, who worked two jobs to provide for my younger sister and me. Similarly, in the book, the brothers returned to their mother in a way that I would look to my mother. My father, however, is White and a veteran who sometimes exhibits behaviors of post traumatic stress disorder from having served in the Korean War and who retired from military service by the time I was 10 years old to work an hourly job. My father's side of the family lived in a rural area in the midwest and I spent the summers playing with my cousins in the countryside. I identified as a female who was often asked why I have a "boy's name," and to this day still receive emails with "Mr." in my greeting. Where were the books that captured the multiple and intersectional aspects of my identity in the 1970s? The answer is that, in my 8-year-old mind, they simply just did not exist.

In this volume, however, not only do the authors show that the books do exist, the authors engage in them in critical ways. Olmstead, Colantonio-Yurko, and Hutchings, Paugh and Acevedo-Aquino, Shelby and Worlds, Pizzo and Rath address literature from an ethnic, racial, and linguistic equity and inclusive perspective. Harrison and Spinelli and Boehm and Worlds problematize Whiteness "as an identity or as a 'state' of being" (DiAngelo, 2011, p. 66), which can impact the lens through which authors represent diversity, how teachers teach diversity through literature, and how readers transact with text to develop an understanding of diversity. Kelly, Tirrito, and Troiani discuss gender identities and suggest how the complexity of those identities are ignored in the language that we use. Finally, Shema explores how the diversity within families is minimalized when they are represented as singular, fixed units composed of a mother, father, and sibling(s). The collection of works encourages teachers to recognize that racism can take different forms and manifest itself in a variety of ways through literature.

Why is It Important to Address Diversity through Literature?

This volume draws from a range of theories to discuss how teachers can use literature to create a narrative that challenges deficit-oriented perspectives to diversity. Deficit-oriented perspectives to diversity refers to an ideology in which differences are compared to dominant and privileged groups of people. In other words, certain groups are marginalized through the presence of barriers that hinder us from seeing any person's or group of people's as successful in comparison to dominant groups. The authors in this volume draw from critical theory, Disability Studies, multimodal theory, and Whiteness Studies, for instance, to painstakingly illustrate an inclusive approach to pedagogy through the use of literature.

For instance, Olmstead, Colantonio-Yurko, and Hutchings write that, as part of a humanizing pedagogy, "students deserve life-affirming texts as part of a humanizing literacy framework in schools" (this volume). Not only does a humanistic perspective to pedagogy disrupt deficit-oriented narratives on diversity, it also views learners as social actors who have agency in their learning. In other ways, if diversity is a range of dynamic and intersectional identities and characteristics, then a humanizing pedagogy is how teachers engage with diversity to create inclusive classrooms.

Harrison and Spinelli discuss creating an inclusive classroom environment through an antiracist pedagogical framework. Boehm and Worlds concur with how antiracist pedagogies "center racism and examine the role of race in inequalities seen both in and out of school" and, as such, literature provides the opportunity to dismantle systematic inequalities built into educational systems.

One such barrier are reading levels. As Olmstead, Colantonio-Yurko, and Hutchings argue, reading levels are often the main mechanism for selecting books for readers. Teachers College Reading Workshop and Fountas and Pinnell center the idea of leveling at the heart of their assessment and curriculum. Leveling, however, can provide a barrier to students reading a range of materials and text complexities. In my research with linguistically diverse students, I have found that students can often read beyond a reading level when allowed to read and retell in a translanguaging context. This has led me, and other researchers (Glasswell & Ford, 2011, Dudley-Marling & Paugh, 2004), to argue that leveling socially constructs notions of not just reading ability, but also of success and failure, if not used correctly and placed within the whole of the curriculum.

Removing the constraints of reading levels allows teachers to open up a range of possibilities with literature to create an inclusive education. If diversity is defined as a range of dynamic states and characteristics, then inclusion can be defined as a way of engaging with diversity. Students can explore mirror texts, discuss social justice issues around race and gender, and how race is connected with positions of power, privilege, and status.

I conclude this preface with a thought about how recognizing privilege and the multiplicity of our identities is part of the roles and responsibilities that we have as teachers and teacher educators. I talked a little about my earlier experiences in school and family life. I, now, live a privileged life as a successful, tenured university professor, but I recognize that that has not always been the case. In some ways, my story should not be one of success based on dominant deficit-oriented narratives. I come from a divorced, low socioeconomic family. Neither of my parents went to college. I certainly did not have it easy in school. In first grade, my teacher made a point of telling my father that I did not know my colors. By the time I was in fifth grade, I was in a remedial reading group. I tell this story because it is through these multiple and varied storylines of my personal and learning autobiography that I read and contemplated the chapters in this book.

I also tell this story because it is the story that our students need to hear. My story is not an idealized story, but one through which I see my role as a teacher educator. That role involves helping my teacher candidates recognize that their students have their own personal histories and experiences. Those personal histories are not always seen in controlled, leveled texts or basal stories that have hidden narratives that promote notions of idealized students. Children and young adult literature, however, holds a breadth of potential in keeping the classroom conversation open and accessible to students of all ages.

References

Arce-Trigatti, A., & Anderson, A. (2020). Defining diversity: A critical discourse analysis of public educational texts. *Discourse: Studies in the cultural politics of education, 41*(1), 3–20.

Beverley, B. (2009). Creating characters with diversity in mind: Two Canadian authors discuss social constructs of disability in literature for children. *Language and Literacy, 11*(1), 1–19. https://doi.org/10.20360/G2201G

Bishop, C. H. (1996). *The five Chinese brothers.* Puffin Books. (Original work published in 1938).

Botelho, M. J., & Rudman, M. K. (2009). *Critical multicultural analysis of children's literature: Mirrors, windows, and doors.* Routledge.

DiAngelo, R. (2011). White fragility. *International Journal of Cultural Pedagogy, 3*(3), 54–70

Dudley-Marling, C., & Paugh, P. (2004). A classroom teacher's guide to struggling readers (pp. 17–36). Portsmouth, NH: Heinemann.

Faist, T. (2010). Cultural Diversity and Social Inequalities. Social Research: An International Quarterly, 77(1), 297–324. https://www.muse.jhu.edu/article/528023.

Glasswell, K., & Ford, M. (2011). Let's start leveling about leveling. *Language Arts, 88*(3), 208–216.

Larrick, N. (1965). The all-white world of children's books. *Journal of African Children's and Youth Literature, 3*(5), 1–10.

Nieto, S. (2015). "Language, literacy, and culture". In *Leaders in critical pedagogy.* Leiden, The Netherlands: Brill.

Noguera, P. A. (2016). Race, education, and the pursuit of equity in the twenty-first century. In *Race, equity, and education* (pp. 3–23). Cham: Springer.

Oluo, I. (2019). *So you want to talk about race.* Seal Press.

Thompson, A. (1997). For: Anti-racist education. *Curriculum Inquiry, 27*(1), 7–44.

Thomson, R. G. (1997). Extraordinary bodies: Figuring physical disability in American culture and literature. Columbia University Press.

Preface

While teaching fourth grade, I shared the picture book Red: A Crayon's Story by Michael Hall with my class. It tells the story of a blue crayon encased in a red wrapper. Everyone in the crayon's life tries to help him be red, instead of blue and offer well meaning suggestions. It isn't until he meets a new friend that he realizes he is not red, but blue. The book touches upon the themes of self-acceptance and respect for others. After a class discussion about the text, I invited my students to further respond in their dialogue journals. One student, Amy (pseudonym), wrote "this is really important to me" and that she liked another student's comment "about people just acknowledging the fact that you're blue and not red." Amy interpreted the message of the book and wrote, "I know people who are like this.Transgendered." She continued by making a connection and sharing a text with me— George by Alex Gino— a chapter book about a young transgendered girl, writing that, "It's about a 4th grader, actually. Her name is George." Amy concluded her reflection with a powerful affirmation, "Don't let anyone steer your personality in the wrong direction."
—Serena's teaching reflection

This classroom scenario above demonstrates how books can open avenues for discussion, reflection, and conversation and act as a catalyst for social transformation in our P-12 and college classrooms.

We, Kathy, an associate professor of Literacy at SUNY Brockport, and Serena, an adjunct associate professor at Queens College and a 5th grade teacher on Long Island, identify as cisgender, White middle-class women, as do the majority of teacher candidates we work with. We recognize that we write and edit this book as white women who generally reflect the demographic statistics of the teaching profession— however, it is for this reason that we need to think about *how* stories are currently represented in the curricula and *whose* stories are represented.

We have called upon our colleagues to help us create this text as a resource to provide both the rationale for engaging in work with inclusive children's and young adult literature and the resources necessary for teachers, counselors, librarians and school administration to incorporate thoughtfully selected literature into the classroom or into school-wide contexts. This volume serves to prepare both teachers and teacher candidates to become reflective practitioners who embrace culturally relevant instruction and who work to ensure inclusion and equity in literacy education.

In collaboration with our colleagues— teacher educators, practicing teachers, a librarian and also a school counselor— we provide multiple perspectives and examples of texts that *open conversations* about powerful topics and ideas that arise in many children's and young adult books. Indeed, it is not enough to just have access to many stories; teachers must consider the ways in which they can engage in discussions around books and their importance. We want to encourage teachers to disrupt curriculum that perpetuates harmful narratives and to interrogate often overlooked ways that schooling spaces silence some stories.

It is our aim to expand upon the use of inclusive and global children's literature to facilitate conversations and enable teachers to provide spaces where all children see themselves, their families and their stories in children's literature, as well as see the many children, many families, and many stories of the world.

How is this Book Organized?

We have organized the book into three sections as follows:

- **Section One Title:** *Embracing Many Stories in the Classroom: Working with Preservice Teachers to Make Conscious Choices about Text Selection*
- **Section Two Title:** *Establishing Inclusive Spaces: Using a Critical Stance to Create Meaningful Practice with Young Adult and Children's Literature*
- **Section Three Title:** *Taking Action: Engaging Students in Literature-Based Discussions for Change*

At the conclusion of each chapter, we offer discussion questions that provide an opportunity for reflection. We invite you, as readers, to consider: How have the stories you've read shaped you? Where have you seen yourself in class curriculum? Which books have helped you understand the lived experiences of others?

Part One Embracing Many Stories in the Classroom: Working with Preservice Teachers to Make Conscious Choices About Text Selection

1. "They are not the common stories that we were told, or that we have been asked to teach": *Re-envisioning Classroom Libraries Through Inclusion of Global Children's Literature*

KATHLEEN OLMSTEAD, KATHLEEN COLANTONIO-YURKO &
MEREDITH HUTCHINGS

Just like Marwan (picture book character), my parents had to leave their home-land, Bhutan, in the middle of the night because of violence and...conflicts. My mom had my older brother when she was 16 years old and the baby was only a month old when she had to leave everything behind and escape the harsh real-ities. My dad had to leave his whole family behind. My parents and some other people fled to Nepal where they lived there for more than 25 years. We lived in a refugee camp and that's where I was born... Life in the camp was good but was not enough to provide food and better education for children. So, my family also decided to leave our camps for American dreams.

—Excerpt, Anna's mirror text reflection

All of our students have stories—some may be similar to Anna's story shared above. But what happens when stories like Anna's are not shared or honored in schooling spaces? According to Short (2012), stories frame how we think about the world and shape our identities—building our intercultural under-standings and our ability to engage in "world making" (p. 9). Stories are intrinsic to our students' development of positive self- identities and world-views, yet we know only some stories are represented on our bookshelves and in our classrooms today. While we, like many other educators, ques-tion "whose stories count?" in the classroom (Cunningham, 2015, p. 21), it is widely acknowledged that the texts available on our bookshelves do not align with the diversity of languages, cultures, and lived experiences of our students—like Anna. This needs to change. All of our students deserve life-affirming texts as part of a humanizing literacy framework in schools.

We also argue that it is not enough to simply have these books on the shelves. We must invite students to question, analyze, and consider representation and authenticity of the story. Making decisions about which books we include and discuss in our classrooms is a political act. By only including some voices, we silence others. As Literacy professors, we began to consider how we engage our own teacher candidates in these discussions around texts and equity. We knew this was particularly important as a survey of our teacher candidates enrolled in their first Literacy course indicated that almost 50% of candidates cited instructional elements like "level" or "reading ability" as the main factor in determining book choices for their students. We wondered how discussions with our teacher candidates could help them move away from what we feel is an overemphasis on socially constructed "levels" that have the potential to marginalize and even "pathologize" children (Dudley-Marling & Paugh, 2004). So, we began to mindfully introduce global children's literature—through immersion in book clubs throughout our teacher education courses to open conversations about equity and representation in Literacy education.

We, Kathy and Kate, are assistant professors of Literacy at a state university in the northeast where the diversity of teacher candidates does not match the diversity of their future students; the majority of our teacher candidates identify as white women. Meredith, a graduate Literacy student and research assistant, joined us in thoughtfully examining the research and in writing this chapter. We all identify as cisgender white middle class women. We recognize that we write this chapter as privileged white women who generally reflect the demographic statistics of the teaching profession; however, it is for this reason that we need to think about *how* stories are currently represented in the curricula and *whose* stories are represented.

The following book chapter addresses how our use of global children's literature supported teacher candidates' understanding of the importance and power of story; particularly stories where students have the potential to see themselves reflected in the classroom. In this chapter we also present the voices of our teacher candidates who have shared reflections of their experiences exploring global children's literature in their introductory Literacy classes (all names are pseudonyms).

The Need for Multiple Perspectives

Kumashiro (2004) suggests students often come to school with harmful partial knowledge, like stereotypes, about others who may be labeled "different." He writes, "when schools do not correct this knowledge, they indirectly allow it to persist unchallenged" (p. xxxvii). Kumashiro's recommendation to educators is to broaden students' understandings of others—"by integrating into the curriculum a richer diversity of experiences, perspectives and materials"(p. xxxvii). We suggest one way to work toward disruption of stereotypes is by incorporating global children's literature into the classroom—allowing students to see the richness and complexity of others' lived experiences as well as their own.

While incorporating global children's literature into the classroom is an excellent way to promote connecting with and having empathy for others, Acevedo (2019) reflects on the consistent lack of diverse literature in many classrooms. As cited in Crisp, Knezek, and Quinn, (2016) and Koss (2015), Acevedo (2019) notes, "The books found in most classrooms reflect a mainstream culture that no longer represents the lives of children and families in those settings" (p. 377).

Inclusive Global Children's Literature

We chose to focus on global children's literature with our own teacher candidates because so many books that we already advocate for and use in our program fall into this emerging category of text. Global children's literature is an inclusive term that can encompass books addressing global culture and texts written about immigrants (Corapi & Short, 2015, p. 6); however, it also "highlights local or national culture, communities, and regions" (Bean, Dunkerly-Bean, & Harper, 2014, p. 241) representing many lived experiences. Global literature differs from multicultural literature—often a term for texts addressing marginalized groups. It also differs from international literature—often a term for texts written by international authors. These terms apply to similar forms of texts; yet, these distinctions are important (Corapi & Short, 2015). We view global literature as a broad, inclusive term that can include additional groups and communities within the United States and around the world (Bean, Dunkerly-Bean, & Harper, 2014) to represent many stories in our classrooms.

Intercultural Understandings and Literature

There is a sense of urgency around students in the United States building an understanding of the world and different cultures. While the notion of children growing-up in an increasingly global society is overused, it is not overstated. According to the Committee for Economic Development (CED) (2006) and Zhao (2010), American schools need to better equip today's students for a competitive global world and workforce by increasing their understanding of different multicultural and global practices and ways of being. Teachers will need to mindfully select and consider global children's literature before they begin to enact practices and develop curriculum for their students for the sake of deeping students' intercultural understanding. Short (2009) explains that "Interculturalism is an attitude of mind, an orientation that pervades thinking and permeates the curriculum" (p. 2). We see global children's literature as an avenue for teachers to support their students in building these deeper layers of cultural understanding and intercultural competence.

Humanizing Pedagogy

Humanizing pedagogy has Freirean roots (Osorio, 2018)—centering children in the classroom and placing value on their languages, cultures and ways of being and knowing in the world. Children's lived experiences and funds of knowledge (Guitart & Moll, 2014) become not only relevant in the classroom, but are considered valued assets. This approach counters what Freire (1970) calls the banking model of education—one in which students are empty and gain knowledge only through the teacher's input—clearly an oppressive educational environment (Moll, Amanti, Neff, & Gonzalez, 1992; Osario, 2018). Incorporating global children's literature honors students' diverse lived experiences while expanding their understandings of others as part of a humanizing framework.

Thinking Beyond Damaging Schooling Practices: Disrupting Leveling as a Main Factor in Book Selection

> In order to achieve humanization, which presupposes the elimination of dehumanizing oppression, it is absolutely necessary to surmount the limit-situations in which men (all people) are reduced to things" (Freire, 1970, p. 93).

While perhaps first initiated with good instructional intentions (Hoffman, 2017), the damaging literacy practice of assigning students reading "levels" results in dehumanization—both within classrooms and across schools.

This misused leveling practice deprives students of their agency (Fountas & Pinnell, 2012) as they are reduced to "things" in what becomes an oppressive literacy environment. Leveling practices are so pervasive, most teachers don't often give them a second thought. The same can also be said of our teacher candidates who may be enculturated into an overemphasis on leveling through their field placement experiences in P-12 classrooms. As mentioned previously, our initial survey of teacher candidates revealed almost 50% of candidates focused on instructional elements like "level" or "reading ability" as the main factor in determining book choices for their students. Perhaps this is also reflective of teacher candidates' own lack of experience with global children's literature in their childhood classrooms. For example, as teacher candidate Mary points out, "Personally, I do not remember seeing or reading many diverse or global books when I was in elementary school." Similarly, Angie reflected, "Many educators may not know about them (global children's books) because *they are not the common stories that we were told, or that we have been asked to teach.*" Therefore, it was increasingly important for us to engage with our teacher candidates in thinking critically about book choice in the classroom. We were able to do this by immersing teacher candidates in a variety of diverse books by establishing global children's literature book clubs.

Creating Spaces for Classroom Conversations: Establishing Global Children's Literature Book Clubs

> We need the transformative power of picture books to open up conversations about our shared world, that connect us to the beautiful, the possible, and the hopeful, and that inspire agency and activism within ourselves and the young people with whom we share texts (Wissman, 2019, p. 15).

As emphasized by Wissman (2019) in the quote above, we value the transformative power of children's literature as well as the safe spaces to interact with others around these texts. Establishing book clubs in our college classrooms both encouraged engagement in deep discussion around a text to consider diverse themes and topics, as well as helped to build a strong passion for reading (Calkins, 2000; Daniels, 1994). Each week new global children's literature books were introduced and teacher candidates met in small groups to thoughtfully discuss and critique the texts. We wanted to "create opportunities for students to think critically about their own identities and perspectives but also to come to a richer appreciation of the humanity of the people represented in the texts" (Wissman, 2018, p. 19). Our ultimate goal was that teacher candidates would be able to reproduce these literacy learning opportunities

with their future P-12 students. Books were selected through use of websites like Social Justice Books https://socialjusticebooks.org/booklists/,
Lee and Low Publishers, who produce books "about everyone for everyone" https://www.leeandlow.com/, and award lists like those from the Jane
Addams Peace Association http://www.janeaddamschildrensbookaward.
org/japa/. We provide brief summaries of some of the texts discussed in
book clubs below:

- *The Name Jar* by **Yangsook Choi**
  This fictional story is based on the author's experiences through the
  eyes of Unhei who moves to a new school in the United States from
  Korea. On her first day, students mock her for her "funny" name, so
  she takes suggestions for a new one but learns to appreciate her name
  and heritage.
- *Those Shoes* by **Maribeth Boelts**
  This picture book depicts the journey of Jeremy and his grandma to
  find the new, popular black and white shoes that all his peers are wear-
  ing. Considering the families' impoverished lifestyle, the author aims
  to open discussion about the difference between wants and needs.
- *Little Leaders: Bold Women in Black History* by **Vashti Harrison**
  This book consists of readings about forty revolutionary and influen-
  tial black women who were activists, athletes, and politicians. Since
  black women are generally underrepresented in literature, the author
  wrote this book to show how black women shaped American history.
- *The Day You Begin* by **Jacqueline Woodson**
  Based on Woodson's uncomfortable experiences being the only black
  girl in an all-white school, she encourages her readers to share their
  lived experiences and embrace the diversity in their world to find
  friends who share their perspectives.
- *Sparkle Boy* by **Lesléa Newman**
  This picture book illustrates a girl Jessie and her brother Casey's love
  of what is sparkly and feminine and how Jessie learns to respect Casey's
  non-binary clothing style. The author strives to open conversations
  about gender expression and conformity in classrooms and households.
- *One of A Kind Like Me/Único Como* Yo by **Laurin Mayeno**
  The book shares a true story about the author's son Danny who wants
  to be a princess in his preschool halloween parade and their journey
  to find his costume. Through this experience, the author's son taught
  her to do what makes one happy regardless of gender roles or other
  people's opinions.

- *Malala, a Brave Girl from Pakistan/Iqbal, a Brave Boy from Pakistan Two Stories of Bravery* by Jeanette Winter
This two-sided book portrays the story of Iqbal, a boy fighting for the end of child slavery and Malala, a girl fighting for girls' education in Pakistan, who were shot during their activism. The author wrote this book to showcase their courage as young activists.

Student Reflections

In reviewing teacher candidates' post book club reflections, we noticed the evolution of a more humanizing framework in their writing. We also observed the growth of candidates' awareness of political and sociocultural classroom perspectives. In the following sections we share two key findings from our examinations of teacher candidates' reflections:

1. Teacher candidates expanded their understanding of meaningful approaches to text selection;
2. Teacher candidates came to value the power of mirror texts.

Below we share the voices of our teacher candidates.

Expanding Understandings of Book Selection

After engaging in global children's literature book clubs, teacher candidates' reflections placed particular importance on opening classroom conversations. Their responses included a greater emphasis on humanizing factors that contribute to classroom book choice. For instance, our teacher candidates noted that books can be selected to:

- "open conversations about inclusivity;"
- "understand others' emotions;"
- "explore empathy;"
- "see other points of view;"
- "show how people should never be excluded."

As teacher educators, we found incorporating these meaningful global children's literature book club exchanges supported our teacher candidates' growth and helped them to interrupt deficit perspectives that might "damage and erase" their future students (Alim & Paris 2017). For instance, teacher candidate Mary reflects,

Children's literature is a great way to introduce different ideas, cultures,

values, and experiences to students to allow them to be open minded and
learn about differences early on. Exposing these ideas to children can create
a world of people who are responsive, aware, empathetic, and respectful.

According to Dyches (2016) many white, middle-class, monolingual teacher candidates do not view themselves as racialized beings. Our work immersing teacher candidates in global children's literature book clubs helped to counter this. For instance, teacher candidate Olive wrote about her growing understanding of herself as a cultural being, and of the privilege she experienced through the book choices provided in the classrooms of her childhood:

> *Prior to this work, I had never realized that most children's books revolved around*
> *white, middle class values because I always saw myself in those books, so I never*
> *thought about it. In actuality, our classrooms are becoming more and more diverse,*
> *so we must provide children with a way for them to see themselves as the characters*
> *in these children's books.*

Similarly, Eliza, another teacher candidate writes:

> *In selecting works for my future students, I aim to find books that show a variety of perspectives, particularly those that may be relevant to students in my class.*
> *Labadie et al. (2012) emphasize the importance of book choices, saying, "we must*
> *find ways to lead them [students] to new ways of understanding the world" (p. 119).*
> *In addition to finding culturally relevant books, it is important to find books that*
> *show multiple viewpoints in order to further students' understandings.*

Additionally, Casey quotes Adichie' s 2009 famous TED Talk emphasizing dangers of a single story:

> *Prior to this course, I did not think about selecting books to give students a global*
> *perspective... One of the most inspiring speakers...explained the notion of a single*
> *story, stating that the purpose of a single story is to "...show a people as one thing,*
> *as only one thing, over and over again, and that is what they become" (Adichie,*
> *2009). The commonalities across different cultures are what unite people and help*
> *to break the idea that differences are too large to relate to one another. They (single stories) are harmful societally because readers grow up believing in stereotypes*
> *depicted about different cultures without gaining greater perspectives. It is important that students understand differing perspectives to function successfully.*

Likewise, Angie writes about the need for the acceptance of multiple identities in the classroom:

> *We need to promote peace and acceptance of others. "The use of culturally relevant texts anchors students' culturally relevant knowledge, such as their identities,*
> *experiences and norms, in ways that improve their literacy outcomes" (Sharma &*
> *Christ, 2017, p. 296).Children and students don't know what they haven't experienced or been taught. If we don't expose them to diversities or things that challenge*

the norms, then those things are looked at as a difference and leads to separation and isolation.

Through immersion in global children's literature book clubs, teacher candidates expanded their understanding about why they need to rely upon diverse books and were able to demonstrate how this will impact their future classroom literacy practices.

The Power of Mirror Texts

Many teacher candidates were struck by the power of mirror texts. A mirror text is a reflection of a reader's experiences and identity, either in the text, illustrations, or a combination of the two (Baldwin, 2018; Sciurba, 2015; Thomas, 2016). When readers engage with a mirror text they "feel a connection that honors and validates their...experiences and stories" (Baldwin, 2018, p. 75). As part of their global children's literature book club reflections, teacher candidates were asked to research and share books they felt were personal mirror texts. We share some excerpts of teacher candidates' mirror text reflections below.

The Need for Multilingual Texts

For some teacher candidates, the global children's literature mirror text assignment allowed them to consider stories they had not encountered in their own educational experiences, but would have liked to. For example, Eliza shared that she never had the chance to see bilingual texts in any of her classrooms, *"English was my second language and I had never encountered a book that is in both English and Polish."* For Eliza, global literature was a rich avenue for her to consider what she would value in her own classroom for her students as she reflects, *"A student whose first language is different than English will only be exposed to books that are either in their language, or English, and barely ever both at the same time."* As a future teacher, Eliza's exposure to global literature resulted in her own reflections on bilingual books in classroom spaces and their importance to students like her. Unfortunately, there is a scarcity of bilingual text produced by publishing companies, making them not easily accessible to teachers and their students (Daly, 2019; Hokenson & Munson, 2014). Teachers like Eliza must make mindful efforts to search for and include bilingual texts in their classrooms. With more diverse learners present in the classroom, bilingual books play a critical role and have significant benefits for English language learners and the classroom community in general (Daly, 2019; Domke, 2018). The incorporation of dual language books in the classroom actively validates bilingual students' native languages in the classroom and has a positive effect on students' social identities (Daly, 2019; Domke, 2018). The thoughtful inclusion of bilingual books within the classroom can represent intersectionality between different lived experiences and foster more positive, affirming attitudes about minority languages within children's literature and classroom communities (Daly, 2019; Domke, 2018).

Seeing Oneself and Others in the Classroom Through Texts
In an experience similar to Eliza, Martha, who self-identifies as Hispanic, noted that she had attended a predominantly white elementary school. She explains, *"My classes weren't very diverse and I did not see any Hispanic children represented in any of the books we read."* Finding a version of *Jack and the Beanstalk* (2006) with a person of color as the protagonist was powerful for Martha. For Martha, books that told traditional tales with characters like her, increased her understanding of how her own students could share in similar, positive experiences. In writing about mirror texts, some teacher candidates reflected that global literature permitted them to consider specific experiences from their own childhood and see other children's experiences reflected back to them. For example, Anna shared the book *Marwan's Journey* (2018) to relate to her own experiences as an immigrant coming to a new country. Anna could see herself in the story and she felt this was encouraging. Yet, Anna emphasized that it was also important for others to understand what could cause someone to leave their homeland and become a refugee. So her mirror text could also be a window text—shedding light on others' experiences (Sims Bishop, 1990).

Another teacher candidate, Louise, shared that it was powerful to read a book about anxiety—a major health issue in the United States (National Institute of Mental Health, 2017). She would have liked to have seen these books in classrooms growing up. For Louise, reading about mental health had a huge impact. Louise reflected, *"When I was a child, I had severe anxiety over the littlest things."* She mentioned that on some days it had a huge toll on her actions. Likewise, teacher candidate Casey, shared that she would have liked to have read and encountered more books in school about children who identified as autistic. *"I remember explaining from a very young age that my brother is different,"* wrote Casey. Casey's brother is autistic and she shared challenges in communicating with friends and others about his disability.

For our teacher candidates, mirror texts, books with characters who resonated with a deep and personal part of their own identity, were a way to expand their own notions of what types of stories were important. Candidate's discussions of which global stories matter went beyond simply diverse texts on shelves, but their desire to have books in classrooms that address and consider distinct human experiences like their own. For example, teacher candidates shared mirror text books that represented their personal lived experiences of living in poverty, growing up with food insecurity, having to wear glasses, having parents that divorced, or a family member with Alzheimer's disease. Candidates came to realize it is not just important to have stories with characters that speak multiple languages or look like our students, it is also important to include stories that feature characters that have a range of human experiences—like stories about emotions and stories that feature discussions of mental health and other personal challenges. These initial searches for mirror texts resulted in a call for including stories in classrooms that demonstrate how people in local, national, and global settings experience and understand a wide variety of issues, topics and life experiences.

Classroom Tips

The book club project provided our students and us an opportunity to reflect on the power of mirror texts and how thoughtfully selected literature permits students to see characters like themselves—characters whose parents fight, characters with disabilities, characters who speak multiple languages, characters who move across the world and go to a new school, characters who can't afford the coolest pair of shoes. And those mirror stories spurred deep conversations and opportunities for reflection about a breadth of critical discussion points from immigration to socioeconomics, and how these issues manifest in schools and contribute to policies and systems of injustice and oppression. Below we provide ideas for teachers to consider to enhance classroom practices.

Text Selection

One of the most challenging aspects of including thoughtful global books in one's classroom is the process of selecting and finding "the right" ones. There exists a multitude of resources that teachers can use to evaluate and consider books for their bookshelves and curriculum. Consider the following:

- Learning for Justice suggests that teachers use their *Reading Diversity Lite: A Tool for Selecting Diverse Texts* to quickly evaluate concepts like representation and authenticity. https://www.learningforjustice.org/sites/default/files/general/Reading%20Diversity%20Lite%E2%80%94Teacher%27s%20Edition2.pdf

- Teachers can use noted book award lists and consult those to see what books are endorsed by different organizations and why.
- We suggest that educators consider following NCTE blogs shared by teachers and researchers who engage in text selection. What texts are they using? Why?
- ILA has a special interest group which gives awards each year to global children's books called: The Notable Books for a Global Society. What books do they suggest? How might you include these texts?

Reading Choice and Book Sharing

Scholars studying reading engagement tout reading choice as an integral factor to promote comprehension and learning (Fraumeni-McBride, 2017). By encouraging students to choose and share their own mirror text books, teachers can provide opportunities for enhancing reading engagement in the classroom while helping kids both see themselves and understand their classmates more deeply. One way to do this is to have students create *mirror text book trailers*—either through designing and orchestrating a live poster presentation or by creating a digital book trailer that can be shared with the class and families.

Mirror Text Book Trailer Directions

1. Initiate a discussion with the question, "What is a book trailer?" Students can begin by deconstructing a popular kids' movie trailer. At the time of this writing, some choices could include the trailers for *Mulan, Moana,* or *Frozen 2*—depending on students' age levels and interests. Teachers can prompt students to consider: Why create a movie or book trailer? What makes an interesting movie trailer? What do trailers include? What do trailers leave out? See more lesson plan ideas for book trailers on readwrite think.org (http://www.readwri tethink.org/). Teachers can also adapt the book trailer rubric found on the website http://www.readwritethink.org/files/resources/les son-docs/30914Rubric.pdf

2. Next, teachers will select a personal mirror text, then model the mirror text selection for students. Teachers can consider and then share—How is this book a mirror text? In what ways do you see yourself in the story? Why did you select this book to share? Students then research a personal mirror text that represents their lived experiences—one they want to share with the class. Next, students create a plan for their trailer— in a format of their choice like a written script or storyboard.

Students list supplies, then work to gather needed items and technology if desired.

3. Trailers can be presented live or students may want to use digital tools (e.g. iMovie trailer, Adobe Spark, Photo Story, etc.) to add visuals, texts, narration and music to produce digital book trailers that can be shared with classmates and families to celebrate the books and create interest in reading.

4. Finally, celebrate book trailer creations and make all books available on display for checking out of the classroom and/ or school library!

Conclusion

If we teach students at a young age that it's ok to like what you like and be who you are then that's what they know and there will be less judgement and more understanding, empathy and acceptance... (As a future teacher), I will be selecting books that "recognize diverse personal and cultural perspectives on an issue and will have a dialogue about that diversity"
(Labadie, Wetzel, & Rogers, 2012, p. 119).

—Excerpt, Angie's reflection

Throughout our time as teachers in both P-12 and college classrooms, we've administered many reading inventories asking students about their reading preferences, experiences, and histories. As teacher educators, we are privileged to hear how the reading experiences of our students—future teachers—influence what they think matters in classroom spaces; how engaging in global children's literature book clubs had an impact on their thinking about classroom text selection. As Sims Bishop reminds us, "When there are enough books available that can act as both mirrors and windows for all of our children, they will see we can celebrate both our differences and our similarities, because together they are what make us all human." (Sims Bishop, 1990, p. xi).

We are encouraged that future teachers like Angie (quoted above) plan to use global children's literature to open conversations to encourage "empathy, understanding and acceptance" in their classrooms to celebrate their students' identities through more thoughtful and more equitable literacy practices. Teachers like Angie can make change in the world one story at a time—and afterall, isn't that the power of a book?

Discussion Questions

1. What books served as mirror texts for you? Why did you find them to be important?
2. How might you provide mirror texts for your own students?
3. What activities might you include to be sure all students see themselves in your classroom?

References

Acevedo, M. V. (2019). Young children playing their way into intercultural understanding. *Journal of Early Childhood Literacy, 19*(3), 375–398. DOI: https://doi.org/10.1177/1468798417727134.

Adichie, C. N. (2009, July). *The danger of a single story* [Video file]. Retrieved from https://www.ted.com/talks/chimamanda_adichie_the_danger_of_a_single_story

Alim, H. S., & Paris, D. (2017). What is culturally sustaining pedagogy and why does it matter? In D. Paris & H. S. Alim (Eds.), *Culturally sustaining pedagogies: Teaching and learning for justice in a changing world* (pp. 1–24).

Baldwin, K. (2018). The power of using international picture books with young children. *Young Children, 73*(2), 74–80. https://brockport.idm.oclc.org/login?url=https://search.ebscohost.com/login.aspx?direct=true&db=eue&AN=129327313&site=ehost-live

Bean, T. W., Dunkerly-Bean, J., & Harper, H. J. (2014). Global and multicultural literature for young adults. In D. McDaniel, M. Koraly, L. Larson, & S. V. Vreede (Eds.), *Teaching young adult literature: Developing students as world citizens.* (pp. 241–262). Thousands Oaks, CA: SAGE Publications.

Calkins, L. M. (2000). A vision for teaching reading: An excerpt from the art of teaching reading. *Creative Classroom, 15*(3), 38–40.

Committee for Economic Development (CED). (2006). *Education for global leadership: The importance of international studies and foreign language education for U.S. economic and national security.* Washington, DC: Author.

Corapi, S., & Short, K. G. (2015, November). Exploring international and intercultural understanding through global literature [Webpage]. Tucson, AZ: Worlds of Words. Retrieved from http://wowlit.org/links/exploring-international-intercultural-understanding-global-literatRre

Crisp, T., Knezek, S. M., Quinn, M., Margaret, B., Giarardeau, K., & Starks, F. (2016). What's on our bookshelves? The diversity of children's literature in early childhood classroom libraries. *Journal of Children's Literature, 42*(2): 29–42.

Cunningham, K. E. (2015). Whose stories count? In *Story: Still the heart of literacy* (pp. 21–50). Portland, ME: Stenhouse Publishers.

Daly, N. (2019). The linguistic landscape of multilingual picturebooks. *Linguistic Landscape, 5*(3), 281–301. https://doi.org/10.1075/ll.18014.dal

Daniels, H. (1994). *Literature circles: Voice and choice in the student-centered classroom.* Portland, ME: Stenhouse Publishers.

Domke, L. (2018). Probing the promise of dual-language books. *Reading Horizons, 57*(3), 20-48.

Dudley-Marling, C., & Paugh, P. (2004). *A classroom teacher's guide to struggling readers* (pp. 17–36). Portsmouth, NH: Heinemann.

Dyches, J. (2016). The trouble with niceness: How a preference for pleasantry sabotages culturally responsive teacher preparation. *Journal of Language and Literacy Education, 12*(2), 9–32.

Fountas, I. & Pinnell, G. (2012). Guided reading: The romance and the reality. *The Reading Teacher, 66*(4), 268–284.

Fraumeni-McBride, J. (2017). The effects of choice on reading engagement and comprehension for second- and third-grade students: An action research report. *Journal of Montessori Research, 3*(2), 19–38

Freire, P. (1970). *Pedagogy of the oppressed.* New York, NY: Continuum.

Guitart, M. E., & Moll, L. C. (2014). Funds of identity: A new concept based on the funds of knowledge approach. *Culture & Psychology, 20*(1), 31–48. doi: https://doi.org/10.1177/135406X13515934

Hoffman, J. (2017) What if "just right" is just wrong? The unintended consequences of leveling readers. *The Reading Teacher, 71*(3), 265–273.

Hokenson, J. W., & Munson, M. (2014). *The bilingual text: History and theory of literary self-translation.* Oxfordshire, EN: Routledge.

Koss, M. (2015). Diversity in contemporary picture books: A content analysis. *Journal of Children's Literature, 41*(2), 32–42.

Kumashiro, K. (2004). *Against common sense: Teaching and learning toward social justice.* New York, NY: RoutledgeFalmer.

Labadie, M., Wetzel, M., & Rogers, R. (2012). Opening spaces for critical literacy. *The Reading Teacher, 66*(2), 117–127.

Learning for Justice. (nd). Reading Diversity Lite. https://www.learningforjustice.org/sites/default/files/general/Reading%20Diversity%20Lite%E2%80%94Teacher%27s%20Edition2.pdf

Moll, L., Amanti, C., Neff, D., & Gonzalez, N. (1992). Funds of knowledge for teaching: Using a qualitative approach to connect homes and classrooms. *Theory Into Practice, 31*(2), 132–141. Retrieved October 31, 2020, from http://www.jstor.org/stable/1476399

National Institute of Mental Health. (2017). Any anxiety disorder [Webpage]. Retrieved from https://www.nimh.nih.gov/health/statistics/any-anxiety-disorder.shtml

Osario, S. (2018). Toward a humanizing pedagogy: Using Latinx children's literature with early childhood students. *Bilingual Research Journal, 41*(1), 5–22.

Sciurba, K. (2015). Text as mirrors, texts as windows: Black adolescent boys and the complexities of textual relevance. *Journal of Adolescent & Adult Literacy, 58*(4), 308–316. http://www.jstor.com/stable/44011164

Sims Bishop, R. (1990). Mirrors, windows, and sliding glass doors. *Perspectives, 1*(3), ix–xi.

Sharma, S.A., & Christ, T. (2017). Five steps toward successful culturally relevant text selection and integration. *The Reading Teacher, 71*(2), 295–307.

Short, K. (2009). Critically reading the word and the world: Building intercultural understanding through literature. *Bookbird: A Journal of International Children's Literature, 47*(2), 1–10.

Short, K. (2012). Story as world making. *Language Arts, 90*(1), 9–17. http://www.jstor.com/stable/41804370

Thomas, E. E. (2016). Stories *still* matter: Rethinking the role of diverse children's literature today. *Language Arts, 94*(2), 112–119. https://secure-ncte-org.brockport.idm.oclc.org/library/NCTEFiles/Resources/Journals/LA/0942-nov2016/LA0942Research.pdf

Wissman, K. K. (2018). Teaching global literature to "disturb the waters": A case study. *English Education, 51*(1), 17–48. https://scholarsarchive.library.albany.edu/eltl_fac_scholar/9

Wissman, K. K. (2019). Reading radiantly: Embracing the power of picture books to cultivate the social imagination. *Bookbird: A Journal of International Children's Literature, 57*(1), 14–25. https://muse.jhu.edu/article/715837/pdf

Zhao, Y. (2010). Preparing globally competent teachers: A new imperative for teacher education. *Journal of teacher education, 61*(5), 422–431.

2. Shifting the Discourse of Expertise Through Engagement With Quality Multicultural and Multilingual Children's Literature

PATRICIA PAUGH & MARIA ACEVEDO-AQUINO

Prioritizing multicultural literature in early childhood classrooms invites important shifts of voice, power, and expertise within those contexts. Yet, there are visible and invisible barriers that prevent such a priority. We, authors Maria and Pat, two university educators, recognized some of these barriers in our own teaching, and engaged in collaborative self-study over five semesters revising what had been a pre-constructed syllabus. Over that time, we reflected and recentered multicultural books in an introductory undergraduate language and literacy course. In this chapter, we share our collaborative actions taken as we revised our course. We begin by defining our approach to teach with multicultural children's literature from a critical and reflective stance. We then present the problems of practice we faced when asked to teach a language and literacy course for pre-service undergraduate students. Following this, we document actions and resulting changes to our teaching as we engaged in reflective practice over several semesters of teaching the course.

Framework for Pre-Service Teachers Learning Through Multicultural/Multilingual Children's Literature

Multicultural children's literature is a designation that holds specific meanings in the field of literacy education. Short, Lynch-Brown, and Tomlinson (2017) describe multicultural literature as books by and about individuals and communities that have been historically marginalized, misrepresented, and underrepresented by the European-American culture in the United States. We approach naming literature "multicultural" with caution, as it can contribute to the maintenance of narrowed understandings of culture that assume cultural beings are those individuals and groups "other than White, European-American" (Botelho & Rudman, 2009, p. xiv). This view is often supported by comments made by White pre-service teachers claiming to have "no culture" (Wang, 2017). Therefore, we view the concept of multicultural literature as a tool for challenging the prevalent single White, European-American story (Adichie, 2009). We embrace the responsibility of creating spaces for pre-service teachers and teacher educators, like ourselves, to interrogate often overlooked diversity within cultural communities, and to recognize when we use our taken-for-granted perspectives and "judg[e] the actions of characters from that positionality" (Short, 2019, p. 8).

The importance of multicultural literature in pre-service education is well documented. When reading multicultural books, pre-service teachers who self-identify as members of marginalized groups, can learn more about their own cultural identities, and see their lives validated by the larger society. They can also develop an appreciation for various contemporary issues within the United States from the perspective of specific cultural communities (Short, Lynch-Brown, & Tomlinson, 2017). Teacher educators have also utilized multicultural literature to support pre-service teachers in exploring their own perspectives on cultural diversity (Howrey & Whelan-Kim, 2009; Iwai, 2013; Jetton & Savage-Davis, 2005; Nathenson-Mejia & Escamilla, 2003), linguistic diversity (Coto & Stewart, 2017), and social issues (Brinson, 2012; Davis, Brown, Liedel-Rice, & Soeder, 2005), as well as the implications of these attitudes and awareness for their future classrooms.

But transactions with multicultural literature can also maintain or create stereotypes, biases and misunderstandings (Cai, 2008). For example, Coto and Stewart (2017) explain that some Latinx readers will have a difficult time making connections to the Latinx body of children's literature that continuously represents stories of immigration, struggles with language(s), and poverty. This pattern in a Latinx collection can contribute to maintaining stereotypical views on specific individuals or communities. With this awareness, we approach multicultural literature with a commitment to read broadly, reflectively, and critically. We understand that books are cultural reproductions situated in specific sociocultural and political contexts (Botelho & Rudman, 2009). As such, we design spaces in our classes to identify, analyze, and interrogate the written text and the illustrations and how they operate to sustain or challenge values, ideologies, and power relations within and beyond communities (Vasquez, Janks, & Comber, 2019).

Situating Children's Literature in a Language and Literacy Class

This chapter describes the evolution of the content and assignments from an undergraduate course focused on language development and literacy in Early Childhood Education. The students were enrolled in the early childhood major at the only public university in a large northeastern city that serves its urban community. These university students and the children they are preparing to teach bring wide-ranging racial, linguistic, cultural, socioeconomic, and experiential diversity to our classes. The university's designation as a Minority Serving Institution (MSI) was reflected in the make-up of the classes. That is, through the years, each class section has had a diverse student population who identified as: Dominican, Puerto Rican, Haitian, Chinese, Vietnamese, American Indian, Iranian, African American, as well as those of mixed-racial and ethnic status. The course was taught by both authors from Fall 2015 through Fall 2019— by Pat, an associate professor and former elementary teacher who identifies as White, female, and Maria, an assistant professor and former preschool teacher, who identifies as Puerto Rican, Latina, and female. When we began teaching the course, the existing syllabus included assignments such as an analysis of children's literature and a shared reading lesson plan designed to support students in integrating children's literature in the classroom as tools for developing children's literacy. As we began teaching our individual sections of this course, we also started talking together, reflecting on our instruction and our students' learning. Early on, we noticed that our intended outcome, for candidates to develop a critical and reflective stance as literacy practitioners, was not carrying over into their assignments.

The assignment that invited us to reconsider our teaching of this syllabus was originally called "Analysis of Children's Literature." This was a written literature review that required students to individually identify three picture books, offer a personal response, and then analyze each book for addressing diversity, child engagement, potential themes, and examples of ways in which each book could be introduced to children. The analysis concluded with an opportunity to compare and contrast the books. The written paper was submitted directly to the instructor. From the start, students were asked to share examples of books they considered important for teaching young children. Old favorites predominated. The overrepresentation of White-European perspectives was obvious. We realized, also, when it came time to write the literature review, students generally continued to choose these same favorites. We were concerned about the lack of diversity in their book selection. We also noted that many of the chosen texts were concept books, rather than rich narrative or informational texts. This latter concern mirrored McGee and Schickedanz's (2007) observations of many early education settings. Like us, these educators found a singular use of concept books addressing letters, colors, fruits and vegetables, and community helpers, among others. While simple concept books have an important role for PreK-2 children's learning, they do not provide experiences with rich and complex ideas. Teachers who include sophisticated picture books as a source of read-alouds engage young children in analytic talk about rich ideas. Guiding young children to engage in analytic and critical talk prepares them to see literacy as an active and transformative process (Souto-Manning, 2009). Thus, it was important to us that we prepared our teacher candidates to challenge their current status quo.

With no designated course on children's literature in this degree program, we began to revise assignments to encourage students to explore new literature and to develop a critical and reflective eye toward stories. First, we renamed the literature review: *Analysis of Multicultural Children's Literature*. With the new name came a new focus on diverse literature, rereadings, and a deeper connection between the course session engagements and the assignment. The updated analysis of multicultural literature highlighted the exploration of issues around authorship, accuracy, authenticity, and representation. Drawing from a transactional view of literacy, explained below, we also emphasized starting from a personal response and moving towards a critical stance. Eventually the paper was substituted with a collaborative peer-reviewed poster presentation session. Below we will elaborate on how we implemented these changes over several iterations of teaching and reflection.

Learning Engagements: Towards a Critical and Reflective Stance

We revised the class sessions to deepen and focus explorations of a range of texts, diverse in topics and depth. These refocused activities introduced and scaffolded routines where the students in the course were encouraged to consider how best to invite young children to participate in literacy learning through the use of quality multicultural children's texts. Specific learning engagements that supported students included: examining their favorites, responding to multimodal professional resources, reading selected multicultural children's literature, and engagement with the literature in meaningful ways.

Rosenblatt's (1995) transactional theory reminds us that each encounter with a text is an opportunity to make new meaning and readers must be encouraged to share personal responses to explore the meaning of the text for their own lives. Influenced by these ideas, we began our journey by exploring multicultural children's literature that the students identified as their favorites on the class survey (completed at the beginning of the course); the ones to which they had strong personal responses. As part of this classroom experience, the students browsed a collection of these favorites, reread them, and shared why or how those became their favorites. Then, they went back to the collection reflecting upon questions like: What kinds of patterns do you notice across these books? What do you notice about the illustrations? What do you know about the authors and illustrators? How do they self-identify? How do these books represent (or not) the cultural and linguistic diversity within the contexts you interact with on a daily basis? The last two questions consistently took the class into a deeper conversation. Sometimes, a few realized that they knew very little about books, authors or illustrators that were representative of the cultural communities that they identified with. The majority of the students realized that their favorite books, authors, or illustrators did not represent the students and children they work with or care for.

At this point we introduced professional multimodal resources to address the importance of representation in children's literature. We watched the TED talk called The Dangers of a Single Story (Adichie, 2009), and examined the Diversity in Children's Literature graphics, created by Sarah Park Dahlen and David Huyck, based on statistical analysis and percentages gathered by the Cooperative Children's Book Center (2019). The students were also introduced to different perspectives on the role of diverse books through the voices of author Grace Lin and Senior Literacy Specialist at Lee & Low Books, Jill Eisenberg. Lin (2016) discussed the importance of Sims Bishop's metaphor on literature as a mirror, encouraging readers to see themselves represented, and literature as windows into new worlds beyond readers' cultural experiences. Eisenberg (2015) challenged myths about diversity in or diversifying early childhood story time, particularly in libraries, and offered strategies for diversifying book sharing with young children.

Throughout the years, some of our students shared their knowledge about majority-group authors addressing diversity. However, most of the students were unfamiliar with the larger field of multicultural children's literature. Since one of the goals was to expose students to rich literature, we developed spaces for them to read selected multicultural children's literature.

We brought books to class representing the following larger communities: African-American, Latino, Asian-/Pacific-American, Arab American and Persian American, American Indian, Religious Cultures, LGBTQAI+, Bilingual books, and stories depicting characters experiencing disabilities (Short, Lynch-Brown, & Tomlinson, 2017). Our particular context invited Haitian-Creole titles like *Mwen damou pou Vava* (Laferriere, 2014), and bilingual Haitian-Creole/English books, such as *Janjak and Freda Go to the Iron Market ale Manche an Fe* (Turnbull, 2013). During interactions like this, some students who were previously silent connected with the content of the literature and took up more participatory roles in the class dialogues. These students facilitated conversations about the importance of translation, as well as issues related to word choice in bilingual books. They also discussed similarities and differences between Haitian-Creole dialects across Haiti that were present in the books. These informal browsings created spaces for students to share their linguistic and cultural expertise challenging dominant discourses of English in the field of early childhood and elementary teacher education programs.

While reading multicultural children's literature is important, readers need to engage meaningfully with the texts in order to connect, reflect, critique, and inquire in significant ways (Short, Lynch-Brown, & Tomlinson, 2017). Two books were particularly effective in supporting students' engagement with rich and complex literature: *The Rooster Who Would Not Be Quiet!* (Deedy, 2017) and *Each Kindness* (Woodson, 2012). Below we share activities that we refocused around these two books to better achieve our goal of deeper student reflection on the inclusion of rich multicultural texts in their teaching of young children.

Re-focused Activity #1: Experiencing Critical Literacy with The Rooster Who Would Not Be Quiet!

The Rooster Who Would Not Be Quiet! (Deedy, 2017) is the story of a rooster who moves into a village/city that is being silenced by the new elected mayor. The rooster is determined to sing, despite the increasingly harsh punishments the mayor imposes on him. The rooster will sing for himself, his family, and others who can't sing. In order to scaffold student engagement, I (author Maria) modeled strategies before, during, and after the read aloud. These included eliciting personal connections, family stories, and predictions with evidence from illustrations and words. For example, examining the repeating onomatopoeia *Kee-kee-ree-KEE!*, written in white font over a bright blue background on the end papers, served as cues for analyzing the integration of Spanish words throughout the story. This onomatopoeia also cued a little game where students spontaneously shared and compared the sounds made by the rooster to sounds in their own primary languages. I also modeled open-ended questions during the read aloud to explore the characters' actions, and asked "why" questions after the reading to think about the meaning of the story for the students.

Each time a reader transacts with a text, they create new meanings (Rosenblatt, 1995). Therefore, multiple encounters with a story are important for significant understandings to be constructed. As such, I created a literacy invitation (Van Sluys, 2005) to scaffold students' thinking about the story and thematically related social issues affecting themselves, children, and families. Literacy invitations are open-ended and flexible. They welcome collaboration, dialogue, storytelling, readers' funds of knowledge, various literacy skills, and deep connections with the story. This invitation encouraged students to think about a moment of silencing and a moment of resistance. The students worked in small groups to create a visual representation of that moment, followed by an explanation of how they connected their selected event with the story. They represented local issues such as the university's incrementation of parking fees and national events like the Dakota Access Pipeline protests and those related to the Black Lives Matter (BLM) grassroot movement. Inspired by BLM, one group wrote:

> We will no longer
> Be silenced for who we are
> United we stand!

The conversations about the images they created, highlighted the importance of selecting rich literature and creating invitational engagements that can encourage readers to connect the books to their lives and to the world.

In subsequent semesters, after participating in the interactive read-aloud activity using this text, students consistently expressed excitement about this story. In author Pat's class several asked to borrow copies of this book to read in classrooms where they were teaching or interning. The theme of voice, and the inclusion of Spanish dialogue, along with the quality of the story, were reasons provided for these requests. This activity demonstrates the potential for involving early childhood teacher candidates as readers themselves. Entering a text as a community of readers provided experiences in what critical reading might look like in their own teaching, and also witness to how a powerful text can provide a complex theme for both young children and adults.

Refocused Activity #2: Focus on the Author for Insight into a Text with Each Kindness

In *Each Kindness* (Woodson, 2012), Chloe and her school friends are ignoring, teasing, and whispering about new arrival Maya, because of how she looks and what she wears (hand me down clothing). Despite Maya's many attempts to befriend her new classmates she is continually rebuffed. As the narrative progresses Chloe is bothered but silently participates in Maya's exclusion. One day, Maya does not return to school, leaving Chloe regretting what she could have done differently. This is one of many powerful books authored by Jacqueline Woodson. The writing and illustrations invite readers to follow what is a direct storyline but one that challenges them to wrestle with complex ideas. Again, as adult readers, our students easily found connections and conundrums related to their own experiences. They also discussed how they would broach the complexity in the book with their young students. Again, several students asked to borrow a copy of the text to read in their classrooms.

Although this text was often used in previous teaching, it became particularly relevant to the course changes during the Fall 2018 semester after Woodson was named National Ambassador for Young People's Literature by the American Library Association. Woodson is an author of color, whose message emphasizes "how books can drive change and instill hope in young readers." (Alter, 2018). Her ambassador role provided a wealth of online resources about her and her work. Sharing the book via a video of Woodson herself reading it aloud attracted student attention. Many students, excited to see an author of color in a position of authority and leadership, were eager to learn more. The next week, I invited them to work in groups with their laptops to further explore Woodson's work. Investigating an author's background and mission is an opportunity to expand teachers' knowledge about their choices of text. For this class, it provided a concrete avenue to challenge the status quo preponderance of White-European authors, characters, and lack of culturally specific contexts still found in the majority of children's books (Short, 2018). As the literature review assignment evolved, it asked for evidence of author research as part of the justification for students' book choices. Figure 1 provides an example of student alignment with their author research. Their rationales often connected to their own lives and identities, as well as issues they projected as relevant to the young children for whom they were responsible. In many cases, investigations unearthed books that were not only new discoveries for the students in my class, but new discoveries for me to add to my own collection. What was poignant in this, was a perceived shift in expertise as students not only asked to borrow Woodson's book for their own use, but brought books with themes aligned with their experiences to educate our class community, including me as the professor.

Book Choices:
Sulwe (Nyong'o)
The Day You Begin (Woodson)
Beautiful (McAnulty)

This student connected with Woodson, choosing her title, *The Day You Begin* as one of the paired texts. She also chose and borrowed *Beautiful* after a classroom browsing session. But the book with the most power for her was *Sulwe*, written about colorism.

Personal connection:
"I chose this book because I feel entirely connected to Sulwe and her experience. Though I've never been compared to night, I have experienced a multitude of colorism growing up. Much like Sulwe, my family is composed of a lot of individuals who have a much lighter complexion than I do. As a child I would always wonder why people who looked like me weren't represented in the media or shown in magazines or books. If I had a book like Sulwe growing up my experiences would have been entirely different. I love how the book can be so gentle while conveying such a deep and problematic topic."

Author connection:
"In such a short, beautiful children's book she (author) completely takes control over society's beauty standards and shows the beauty in being both dark and light. I believe this book can be beneficial for all students regardless if colorism has directly impacted their lives. The book celebrates uniqueness and acceptance and carries a powerful message that all need to hear."

Figure 1: Student Project Sample

Participatory Poster Event

During the Fall of 2017, one student noted with regret that there was little time in the course to learn more about her peers' chosen texts. Reflecting on this student's comment, I (author Pat) realized that the written paper assignment could (and should) be more of a learning opportunity for all. In subsequent semesters the literature review shifted from a paper to a collaborative poster event. Students worked as partners to investigate a picture book that would be relevant to children they were or would be teaching. They were asked to create and present a multicultural analysis of this text as well as two additional multicultural/multilingual texts that paired thematically. The criteria for their posters built on those from the paper, with some enhancements such as the author investigation discussed above. They were asked to research not only the authors, but tap resources on relevant children's books by browsing links such as the Worlds of Words: Center for Global Literacies and Literatures (https://wowlit.org/). Students browsed and some borrowed books from collections I brought to class. Preparation for the poster also included a focus on the role of visuals and placement of text. This activity connected to another class activity, analyzing illustrations in the children's literature, based on Molly Bang's art principles (Bang, 1991) and included analyzing some web resources on visual communication, especially sample conference posters.

The poster conference itself consisted of two sequential events where students responded by filling out a conference template that was handed in as part of their assignment grade. The first event was a Gallery Walk. After setting up their own posters, students circulated and viewed all posters. There was room on their conference template to list several books that would be a good fit for their own students and provide a rationale for their choices. This was a way to view all the choices and to consider some that would be responsive to their own teaching context. The second event was the Paired Peer Review where each set of partners was assigned to present to, as well as assess, with one other student team. The second part of their conference template was based on the assignment rubric and they became peer assessors. Peer assessors were asked to look for and provide written feedback about the following areas: (1) culture, power, and perspective in the text and illustrations; (2) supplemental sources such as author information online or personal conversations with a teacher or librarian who used the text; (3) the relevance of the paired texts to the overall theme; and (4) the quality of the visual presentation. They were encouraged to interact through questions and discussion with the paired team.

Over both years of the conference, the student posters were artfully created and well documented. The displays indicated rich choices of texts and analysis around the required criteria. The example shared in the previous section featuring the text *Sulwe* (Nyong'o, 2019) (Figure 1) demonstrated one connection to the theme and to an author. Another example featuring the book *Two white rabbits* (Buitrago, 2015) provided insights into culture, power, and perspective. *Two* white Rabbits was chosen for review in both 2018 and 2019 by students who were primary Spanish speakers. It is the story of a father and daughter who together are making the journey north from Central America across the US border. The reviewers chose both the Spanish and English versions of this story. On the posters, they highlighted the importance of issues involving immigration experiences, rationalizing that many young children in local classrooms directly experience this topic: either as refugees themselves, through interactions with school peers, or as witnesses in public discourse such as media or adult conversations. One presenter explained:

> I chose this book because I like having the book in English and Spanish. I also found the subject interesting, there are many children in the classrooms who go through this and it is a good book to introduce and with which many will feel identified. Sometimes parents find it a bit difficult to explain this topic at home, this book and others tell stories that are very much related to immigrants and the kids can understand better. Both stories humanize immigrants and their experiences...for immigrants...see themselves in a positive light...for readers who are not personally familiar...these books can build empathy by humanizing experiences that immigrant children frequently endure particularly those who cross into the United States without documentation. All in all...any and every child should read.

Both of these presenters also engaged more visibly during classes leading up to the conference as we reviewed books, such as the rooster text, that featured their primary language, Spanish. This valuing of languages other than English was another reason shared for their choosing *Two White Rabbits*. The other presenter stated:

> Cultural diversity is also an ongoing issue. The idea that this story is written in Spanish and translated in many different languages gives children of all races ability to relate to the story, whether or not they themselves are immigrants.

Searching across text for themes relevant to young children's lives also produced increasingly thoughtful rationales for book choices. In another example, a team chose three texts related to the theme of empathy. Choices included: *Thank You Mr. Falker* (Polacco, 1998), *Back to Front and Upside Down* (Alexander, 2012), and *A Shelter in Our Car* (Gunning, 2004). An earlier class discussion had pinpointed kindness and empathy as vital in developing compassion for others as this can be invisible in most media encountered by young children. This team summarized their rationale:

> These three texts create a space for compassion and empathy. In all three the character finds a champion that helps them feel safer and more empowered. Through storytelling the struggles of each child is poignant and helps the reader to feel what they feel, think what they think, experience what they experience. Empathize.

The level of care and time students spent at the conference was impressive. Students were cognizant of being careful and supportive of each other. They did not rush out at the end of the session despite the late hour. Several students stayed overtime to complete their reviews carefully. One pair laughingly noted, "We are Haitian and Haitians help others." This is another example of the shift in authority and ownership within the classroom community; a shift noted not only here but collectively across the activities described above.

Final Reflections

Vasquez (2014) reminds us that "incorporating a critical perspective into our everyday lives as teachers is therefore about living critical literacies by experiencing firsthand what it would mean to take on this perspective as a way of framing our participation in the world" (Vasquez, 2014, p. 1). Through collegial reflection and revising of this language and literacy course, we educated each other and simultaneously we noted an evolution in our students' learning. First, there was a greater awareness around the existence of new voices in children's books; Second, some students who were previously silent connected the content of the literature and became more vocal and participatory. In conjunction with these shifts, the participation structures in class became more dialogic; Third, the change in mode to the collaborative poster session tapped previously invisible resources. Students expressed themselves through visual as well as written media and as they looked to each other as experts. While young children can engage critically with texts, the educators around them must guide them through this journey. Living the critical engagements in texts was important for our early childhood candidates. We feel more confident in our efforts to prepare them to more purposefully engage the children around them.

Discussion Questions

1. Reflect on three picture books that you regularly use in your classroom or that are "personal favorites". Consider the questions posed by the authors: What kinds of patterns do you notice across these books? What do you notice about the illustrations? What do you know about the authors and illustrators? How do they self-identify? How do these books represent (or not) the cultural and linguistic diversity within the contexts you interact with on a daily basis?

2. Evaluate your classroom library. Is it a place to "create spaces for students to share their linguistic and cultural expertise?" If not, which titles or authors could you consider to allow for a multilingual experience?

References

Adichie, C. N. (2009, July). The danger of a single story [Video]. https://www.ted.com/talks/chimamanda_adichie_the_danger_of_a_single_story

Alter, A. (2018, January 4). National Ambassador for young people's literature. *The New York Times*. https://www.nytimes.com/2018/01/04/books/jacqueline-woodson-is-named-national-ambassador-for-young-peoples-literature.html

Bang, M. (1991). *Picture this: How pictures work*. Sea Start.

Botelho, M. J., & Rudman, M. K. (2009). *Critical multicultural analysis of children's literature*. Routledge.

Brinson, S. (2012). Knowledge of multicultural literature among early childhood educators. *Multicultural Education*, Winter, 30–33.

Cai, M. (2008). Transactional theory and the study of multicultural literature. *Language Arts, 85*(3), 212–220.

Cooperative Children's Book Center. (2019, November 21). Publishing statistics on children's/YA books about People of Color and First/Native Nations authors and illustrators. https://ccbc.education.wisc.edu/books/pcstats.asp

Coto, M., & Stewart, M. A. (2017). Literatura multicultural en Español: ¿Abriendo ventanas o reforzando estereotipos? *Journal of Latinos and Education, 16*(2), 156–163.

Davis, K., Brown, D. G., Liedel-Rice, A., & Soeder, P. (2005). Experiencing diversity through children's multicultural literature. *Kappa Delta Pi Record*, Summer, 176–179.

Eisenberg, J. (2015, October 5). 6 Myths about Diversity in Early Childhood Storytimes (and How We Can Read Diverse Books in Our Library's Storytime Now). http://test18.demcoideas.com/blog/6-myths-diversity-early-childhood-storytimes/

Howrey, S. T., & Whelan-Kim, K. (2009). Building cultural responsiveness in rural, preservice teachers using a multicultural children's literature project. *Journal of Early Childhood Teacher Education, 30*(2), 123–137.

Iwai, Y. (2013). Multicultural children's literature and teacher candidate's awareness and attitudes toward cultural diversity. *International Electronic Journal of Elementary Education, 5*(2), 185–198.

Jetton, T., & Savage-Davis, E. M. (2005). Preservice teachers develop an understanding of diversity issues through multicultural literature. *Multicultural Perspectives, 7*(1), 30–38.

Lin, G. (2016, March 18). The windows and mirrors of your child's bookshelf | Grace Lin | TEDxNatick. https://ed.ted.com/on/a0o0BODb

McGee, L., & Schickedanz, J. (2007). Repeated interactive read-alouds in preschool and kindergarten. *Reading Teacher, 60*(8), 742–751.

Nathenson-Mejia, S., & Escamilla, K. (2003). Connecting with Latino children: Bridging cultural gaps with children's literature. *Bilingual Research Journal, 27*(1), 101–116.

Rosenblatt, L. (1995). *Literature as exploration*. Modern Language Association of America.

Short, K. G. (2018). What's trending in children's literature and why it matters. *Language Arts, 95*(5), 287–298.

Short, K. G. (2019). The dangers of reading globally. *Bookbird, 57*(2), 1–11.

Short, K. G., Lynch-Brown, C., & Tomlinson, C. (2017). *Essentials of Children's Literature* (9th ed.). Pearson.

Souto-Manning, M. (2009). Negotiating culturally responsive pedagogy through multicultural children's literature: Towards critical democratic literacy practices in a first grade classroom. *Journal of Early Childhood Literacy, 9*(1), 50–74.

Van Sluys, K. (2005). *What if and why? Literacy invitations for multilingual classrooms.* Heinemann.

Vasquez, V. (2014). *Negotiating critical literacies with young children* (10th ed.). Routledge.

Vasquez, V., Janks, H., & Comber, B. (2019). Critical literacy as a way of being and doing. *Language Arts,* 96(5), 300–311.

Wang, Y. (2017). A bridge to intercultural understanding: Reading teachers in the U.S. & English learners in China read children's literature books in a global book club. *Multicultural Education,* Fall, 41–47.

Children's Literature

Agra Deedy, C. (2017). *The Rooster who would not be quiet.* Scholastic.

Alexander, C. (2012). *Back to front and upside down.* Eerdmans Books for Young Readers.

Buitrago, J. (2015). *Two white rabbits.* Groundwood.

Gunning, M. (2004). *Shelter in our car.* Children's Book Press.

LaFerriere, D. (2007). *Mwen Damou pou Vava.* Educa Vision.

McAnulty, S. (2016). *Beautiful.* Running Press Kids.

Nyong'o, L. (2019) *Sulwe.* Simon Schuster Books for Young Readers.

Polacco, P. (2001). *Thank you Mr. Falker.* Philomel Books.

Turnbull, E. (2013). *Janjak and Freda go to the iron market.* Light Messages Publishing.

Woodson, J. (2012). *Each kindness.* Nancy Paulsen Books.

Woodson, J. (2018). *The day you begin.* Penguin Young Readers Group

Part Two *Establishing Inclusive*
Spaces: Using a Critical
Stance to Create Meaningful
Practice with Young Adult
and Children's Literature

3. Embracing Our Students' Stories Through a School-Wide Book Club

GINA KELLY, PAMELA TIRRITO & SERENA TROIANI

Story enables us to encounter experiences and engage in dialogue about all that contributes to the connectedness and differences of our lives. Providing opportunities for our students to engage in conversations that may prove difficult gives them the tools to make informed decisions about the world they live in (Vasquez, 2007). In this chapter, we, Gina (school counselor), Pam (reading teacher), and Serena (fifth grade teacher), all identify as White, cisgender females. We present the development and execution of our elementary school wide book club (book club) where we serve as co-chairs. We begin with a discussion of critical literacy theory and how it informs the book club. We continue with the history and functions of the book club including how books are selected and ultimately shared. An emphasis is placed on the most recent school years, where LGBTQ+ needs at the elementary level led to a focus of picture books that addressed the topic. We end with a selected bibliography of books and paired activities as well as a list of additional recommended resources.

Building a Critically Literate Community

The book club was formed approximately ten years ago by Gina to address the need for character education and to meet the social emotional needs of our students while embracing the diversity of the school community. The aim was to provide a way to create a more empathetic community of citizens (Greene, 1995). The origins of the book club have evolved to operate within a critical literacy framework and instructional stance to address the monologic exposure, or one point of view, many of the children experience. We aimed to move to a more dialogic environment, one where students are enabled to engage in conversation using the resources made available to them, contributing to the expansion of their understandings of one another, themselves, and the world (Freire, 1970/2009; Stock, 1995). Vasquez et al. (2019) provide key tenets of critical literacy theory describing it as involving the understanding and questioning of sociopolitical systems. The authors explain how critical literacy practices are transformative, contributing "to changing inequitable ways of being and problematic social practices" and to creating spaces that engage "learners in powerful and pleasurable ways" that take on these issues while achieving a better life for all (Vasquez et al., 2019, pp. 307–308). It is within these tenets that we frame the purpose of the book club. Our goal is that the children will be able to view a variety of topics and issues, and see the possibilities of improvement or change while engaging in dialogue that cannot be ignored (Leland et al., 1999; Luke, 2012; Vasquez, 2007).

Critical messages, shared in a friendly, picture book format provide an opportunity for the children to expand their understanding of the world, and the notion of acceptance for all. In line with Bishop's (1990) conclusion of books as mirrors, windows, and sliding glass doors, and Laminack and Kelly's (2019) discussion of books as bridges, the literature provides an opportunity for the children to see themselves through reflection, and experience others by looking into a world they may never have witnessed before, all while allowing them to traverse across experiences, understandings, and thoughts.

The Formation and Functionality of the School-Wide Book Club

All faculty and staff members were invited to be part of the book club committee. The inclusion of all was important to make it as diverse as possible in both talents and identity. The committee has since developed to approximately fifteen members, including us as co-chairs, consisting of teachers and staff across grade levels and varying disciplines. The book club committee as a whole is primarily represented by White females, which is a common demographic in many school settings. Being aware of our identities and privileges, we take seriously our charge of researching picture books appropriate for the varying maturity levels of our kindergarten to fifth grade students while acknowledging the paramount importance of selecting texts that represent, address, and embrace diversity. We also consider the social emotional learning in our school building with the goal of positively shifting and impacting the school culture. We aim to select books that are relatable and understandable with a message that is not lost on our younger population, and remains engaging for our older students.

The committee is also responsible for the presentation of the books at school wide assemblies and for the creation of activities that support critical engagement with the literature. Originally, the committee selected six books each year. That number has since decreased to four in response to the budget and time constraints of increased curriculum standards and statewide assessments. The committee meets approximately six times a year; initially at the conclusion of a school year to share found texts to be considered for the following school year. The final list is provided to the principal who uses budget funding to purchase the picture books for each classroom teacher and support staff. During the first month of school, the committee meets to establish dates to share the selected books, ensuring that there are no school or community wide events that may coincide. Approximately four to six weeks prior to the scheduled assembly, the committee meets to plan the presentation of the book as well as the accompanying activities. Additionally, a letter is drafted to distribute to the students' families emphasizing the bridge between the home and school. This letter includes the book selection, a brief description of the text, and the subsequent activity students will participate in. The letter also indicates whether the activity will take place in school or at home and then returned to be shared with the school community (See Appendix A and B for a sample).

Throughout the history of the book club, texts emphasizing a variety of topics or themes, such as acceptance, tolerance, diversity, courage, and mindfulness, have been presented. The selected books are distributed to classroom teachers and staff approximately one week prior to the scheduled school assembly. Teachers are encouraged to share the book in their classroom to provide time for a more intimate discussion of the text. Suggested activities are completed in individual classrooms or sent home as a "homework assignment". At the assembly, a pre-selected staff member reads aloud the book while it is displayed on a large screen for all of the students to see. An accompanying presentation that is related to the story or its theme often occurs as is a selection of completed activities by the students to highlight the message in the book and provide a sense of commonality amongst the students. At times, the singing of a song led by the school music teacher rounds out the assembly. The selected bibliography list at the conclusion of this chapter highlights those activities.

Exploring Gender Diversity through Literature

During the 2018–2019 school year we saw an increase in the number of students who identified with a variety of gender identities. As a committee, and with the support of our principal, we decided to focus on gender diversity, identity formation, and acceptance of the self and others. Addressing LGBTQ+ needs is imperative and research has shown that elementary students are ready to learn about gender diversity just as much as other social issues (Hartman, 2018; Möller, 2020; Ryan et al., 2013;Vasquez, 2007).

There was a concern among some teachers that there would be push back from parents as well as an implied perception from some staff that "pushing of beliefs" or "trying to convert people," was the goal, rather than awareness of others actions and their effects on people, especially the most vulnerable, our students. The Learning for Justice Best Practices for Serving LGBTQ Students guide (2018), discusses the role of teachers as change agents who advocate for the rights of all students. They address the importance of "an inclusive and empowering environment" where "meaningful, constructive, and rewarding social, emotional and academic learning can take place for everyone involved" (p. 18).

Several faculty and staff meetings were dedicated to learning more through workshops provided by LGBTeach to "foster awareness, inclusivity, and reflection"(www.LGBTeach.org) about the LGBTQ+ community. The workshops focused on opening conversations, dispelling myths and misunderstandings, exposure to vocabulary, and providing safe spaces for faculty and staff to ask questions, advice, and seek guidance.

A book club for the faculty and staff, led by the principal and assistant principal, was also established as an additional form of professional development. Approximately thirty faculty and staff members read the book *Becoming Nicole: The Transformation of an American Family* (Nutt, 2016), the biographical story of a family and their experiences as their transgender child transitioned. Biweekly morning book club conversations allowed time for honest discourse, compassion, and reflection. It is the responsibility of public school educators to provide learning environments where all children are valued, to affirm LGBTQ+ identities in schooling spaces, and to frame LGBTQ+ topics as educational issues (Payne & Smith, 2011; Rands, 2009; Staley & Leonardi, 2019). By engaging in the literature and professional development together as an entire school community, we were able to address concerns and inquiries while encouraging our students and staff to be empathetic, understanding, and inclusive.

The support of the school administrative leadership was necessary for us to successfully move to addressing the need for gender equity and creating a book club that affirmed LGBTQ+ identities in our school. In order for our students to be well rounded learners, it was crucial to have the entire staff and community sharing in some common education where, "learners become teachers of their understandings and experiences, and teachers become learners of these same contexts" (Luke, 2012, p. 7).

We looked for the literature and subsequent activities to move beyond the walls of our school building recognizing that it could be the catalyst for true change (Rice, 2002; Ryan et al., 2013). The literature became a vehicle for our school community to either see a reflection of themselves or to learn more about others, resulting in a community that strives for kindness, acceptance, expanding understanding of norms, and each other's beliefs.

Book Club in Action

As discussed, the 2018 and 2019 school year book selections focused on addressing LGBTQ+ inclusion Picture books were chosen that addressed LGBTQ+ identity in a way that reflected age and experiences of the children, while providing a window for them into the experiences of some of their classmates.

The year began with *They All Saw a Cat* (Wenzel, 2016). This picture book explores the different perspectives one has when viewing the same animal. From a dog, to a fish, to a human and then from the perspective of self, this book demonstrates how our personal experiences contribute to our understanding of others. After sharing the text, brain teaser images (ambiguous images/reversible figures) were displayed on a large screen. The children were asked to raise their hand if they could see a specific image. The children's reactions indicated whether or not their "vision" gave them the impression that was being asked. When the second image was provided, it was clear by the reactions of the students how the ambiguous image led to confusion in their thoughts. The lively exchanges between them was indicative of the communication taking place and the understanding that alternative viewpoints were being seen. This interaction provided an opportunity to reinforce among the children how our experiences shape the world we see, and that our eyes all see things from the monologic experiences we have had. By sharing the reversible figures, the children were provided with a dialogic experience, (Freire, 1970/2009), one where the discussion was led and guided by their observations and inquiries. To further their exposure, a bulletin board was created in the main hallway of the school that contained additional ambiguous images. As classes and students passed they were provided with an opportunity to discuss and share which image(s) they saw.

Our second book choice, *Sparkle Boy* (Newman, 2017) embraces acceptance, respect, and the freedom to express yourself by telling the story of a pair of siblings; a boy who loves all things sparkly and his older sister who is confused by his interests.

The book was shared in the classroom prior to the assembly, providing an opportunity for children to discuss in a small group setting the themes that were presented throughout the book, including gender stereotypes. Students in grades K – 5 were provided with a reader response activity to the questions "What does it mean to be yourself?" and "What does it mean to have family support for something that's important to you?". Classroom teachers asked children if they were comfortable sharing their responses and with their permission, their statements were shared anonymously during the assembly.

Examples of some of the childrens' responses are as follows:

- *"Being yourself means that you are your own person and you have your own ideas and thoughts"* (3rd Grade)
- *"It does not matter if you are different than other people. It is fine if girls wear sports stuff. It does not matter. Maybe boys like to play with dolls. It does not matter. Be yourself."* (5th Grade)
- *"To have a family that supports me is when I come home and tell my parents that something bad happened my parents would tell me to stand and tell some [one] I could and it really helps me"* (3rd Grade)
- *"To have family support means to have someone that has your back. It is important to have a reliable person at your side."* (5th Grade)

The book permitted us to use critical literacy questions and ideas that allowed for the questioning of representation in the text, our school, and the community. Providing opportunities for students to make connections to texts, their lives, and the world around them promotes positive identity development (Learning for Justice, 2018). These samples of childrens' responses to the questions posed are reflective of the positive identity development that text connections provide. In addition to sharing the story and the children's responses, children and staff were encouraged to dress in their most "sparkly" clothes for the assembly in an attempt to "break" those stereotypes.

Our third book choice, *Red: A Crayon's Story* (Hall, 2015) touches upon many themes including self acceptance and respecting others by telling the story of a blue crayon encased in a red wrapper. While everyone in his life tries to help him be red and offer well meaning suggestions, it isn't until a new friend helps him realize that he is indeed blue.

After reading the story in their classrooms, students were provided with a crayon template from Welcoming Schools, a Human Rights Campaign Foundation (https://assets2.hrc.org/welcoming-schools/documents/WS_

Lesson_Red_A_Crayons_Story.pdf).This template gave children in grades K – 2 an opportunity to respond to the prompts "I Like", "I Don't Like", and "I Feel". Students in grades 3 – 5 were provided with a blank template where they were encouraged to share stories of what someone would not know about them by looking at them. As with *Sparkle Boy*, children were asked prior to the assembly if they were comfortable sharing their work anonymously. The following are some of those responses.

One kindergartener provided the following three responses:

- *I like has* (hearts)
- *I don't like gun*[s]
- *I feel happy*

One second grader provided the following three responses:

- *I like to play with girl toys*
- *I don't like to play on playgrounds*
- *I feel that people will make fun of me because I am a boy*

One fourth grader provided the following three responses:

- *Someone that looks at me might not know I have two moms*
- *Someone that looks at me might not know that I am afraid of cats*
- *Someone might not know that I play golf*

One fifth grader provided the following response:

- *When I got to school in the U.S. for the first time I looked happy but was really feeling nervous and scared*

The students' responses reflect their ability to emphasize that an outwardly appearance does not provide insight to an individual's personal identity, inner thoughts, and experiences. Their responses were supported by illustrations emphasizing their experiences and what they were expressing, all indicators of positive identity development. The opportunity to respond to the text individually and be reflective of others' comments provided a space for the children to relate sympathetically while allowing for expressions of empathy and understanding.

Our final book for the school year was *I Am Enough* (Byers, 2018), which presents a message of acceptance of the self and others in a poetic form. Readers follow the positive affirmations that address the need for self-esteem, and respecting and being kind to others. After sharing the story in their classroom, students were provided with an activity retrieved from the Harper Collins website (https://www.harpercollins.com/9780062667120/i-am-enough/). Students in grades K-2 were presented with the template "With a Little Help from my Friends" which included an outdoor scene of children. The students were prompted to illustrate playing with their friends. Many of the children's illustrations included self images and their friends participating in various outdoor activities. Important to note was the childrens' use of captions and phrases to support the actions and expressions within the illustration.

Third through fifth grade students were provided with a template from Harper Collins (https://b0f646cfbd7462424f7a-f9758a43fb7c33cc8adda 0fd36101899.ssl.cf2.rackcdn.com/activity-guides/AG-9780062667120. pdf) titled "I Am ..." prompting them to complete the following statements forming poetic sentences identifying what makes them unique.

- My eyes are...
- I like to...
- My hair is...
- I live in...
- My favorite color is...
- I am...

One student's completed poem read as follows:

My eyes are observant.
I like to make people feel happy when they are sad.
My hair is a thing I like about myself.
I live in a world with great people.
My favorite color is a color that I wear a lot.
I am happy for who I am.

Another student's completed poem read as follows:

My eyes are filled with joy.
I like to be myself.
My hair is the way I like it.
I live in a neighborhood of respect.
My favorite color is the colors of joy.
I am unique.

The students' completed illustrations and poems are evidentiary of positive self-esteem and self-acceptance. Their expressions provided an opportunity for their peers to "see" the feelings, thoughts, and experiences of others and perhaps a reflection of themselves in the work.

Building upon addressing the needs of LGBTQ+ students, the 2019–2020 book selections continued to emphasize inclusion and acceptance with the knowledge that "change can begin with children's literature" (Rice, 2002, p. 40). Our goal was to continue to create spaces where critical literacy could be lived, engaging our learners in conversations that should not be ignored, while helping them understand social issues around them (Vasquez, 2007; Vasquez et al., 2019).

The first book, *Be Kind* (Zietlow Miller, 2018), powerfully expresses through the thoughts and actions of the protagonist the message that small acts of kindness, although not always easy, matter and make a difference. Children were provided with an individual kindness banner where they indicated how they can be kind to themselves, at home, and at school (https://www.teacherspayteachers.com/Product/What-Does-it-Mean-to-be-Kind-Book-Companion-3575009). The banner was modified to illustrate a gender neutral child and for Kindergarten students who illustrated the statement "I Can Be Kind". The completed banners were displayed in classrooms and throughout the school hallways, providing an opportunity for students to reflect on the various ways they can spread kindness to others and for themselves. The following are examples of some students' work.

- Kindergarten – included an illustration of himself and a friend with an apple in hand. The teacher recorded, "I can share an apple with a friend".
- First grade – "*I Et vechbls*" (I eat vegetables); "*I Woch Dichis*" (I wash dishes); "I *Hep a cndrgrdn*" (I help a kindergartener).
- Third grade – "*I can be kind to myself by eating healthy so I don't get sick*"; "*At home I can be kind by helping my sister take out the dishes from the dishwasher*"; "*I can be kind at school by sitting with someone that is sitting alone*".
- Fifth grade – "*I can be kind to myself by eating good things and doing good things for my body*"; "*I can be kind at home by helping around the house and doing things without being asked*"; "*I can be kind at school by standing up for everyone and cheering friends up when they are down*".

The second book, *Strictly No Elephants* (Mantchev, 2015) presents the effects of exclusion when certain pets are restricted from a club, and the benefits of an inclusionary club where all are welcome. Classroom teachers were encouraged to have their class create a poster using the prompt, "You want to welcome everyone to our school. How can you do that in a poster?" Completed posters were displayed in the school cafeteria/auditorium prior to the assembly. The colorfully decorated student posters included welcome messages in varying languages, such as "Shalom", "Konnichiwa", "Guten Tag", "Hola", "Ciao" and "Ni Hao", as well as phrases, such as "Never Be A Bully", "Welcome Everyone", "Be Nice", "Include Everyone", and "I Love a Little More Each Day".

The childrens' participation with the literature and the subsequent activities are indicative of the need for critical literacy practices. The responses through their words and illustrations provided real-world connections and transformative opportunities for them and their peers. Through engagement with the literature, they were able to connect their identities and experiences. These opportunities enabled them to learn to make informed decisions, while thinking and acting ethically (Vasquez et al., 2019).

An Interruption: The COVID-19 Crisis

The remaining two book selections, *Perfectly Norman* (Percival, 2017), the story of a young boy whose wings make him feel miserable, and *When You Are Brave* (Zietlow Miller, 2019), a story that reaffirms the spark of courage we all have within us, were unable to be shared due to the COVID-19 pandemic that resulted in schools moving to an emergency online platform.

Perfectly Norman (Percival, 2017) was slated to be shared in April. The intent was to create a life size display of wings in the main school hallway for children to stand in front of and have their picture taken. Each feather of the wing would contain an affirmation statement by individual students and staff members. *When You Are Brave* (Zietlow Miller, 2019) was slated to be shared in June with the intent of connecting it to a potential fundraiser. Plans had not been finalized.

Discussion was made about possibly sharing the books remotely through teachers' individual Google Classroom websites. Additional thoughts included pre-recording a "book club assembly" to share remotely. The decision was made to not share the books due to two contributing factors; the first being the concern that the weight of the books' messages may be lost through an online presentation. The second concern regarded funding as the COVID-19 crisis had an impact on school budgets. The possibility and likelihood of a reduction in funding may result in the inability to purchase new books for the 2020–2021 school year. It was decided that it would be best to hold on to these stories ensuring that two books would be available to share school wide during the 2020–2021 school year.

The consideration for lack of funding prompts the need to discuss how a book club can be created with limited resources. Knowing that budget cuts are always looming and many educators are working in districts where there would be no funds available to support this exact model of a book club, we offer the following suggestions on how you can recreate this extremely powerful program with no funds.

- Read alouds of stories are available on websites such as YouTube, SchoolTube, and author and publishers' websites.
- A single copy can be retrieved from your local or school library and distributed amongst classrooms on a rotating schedule.
- Many book companion activities can be accessed for free at publishers' or authors' websites or can be created/designed by faculty.

Having the physical book for all classrooms is ideal but not necessary. Teaching the message from the literature is the ultimate goal.

Conclusion

The formation and execution of the book club emphasizes our understanding of supporting and developing the social and emotional learning experiences of our students while engaging in critical literacy discussions. Sharing students' individual stories and exposing them to the valuable experiences of others within their school community and the community at large, helps students recognize and embrace the similarities and differences among them. The childrens' engagement with and responses to the texts indicate that they are ready to participate in conversations that are important and impact their lives (Vasquez, 2007). Their illustrations and words reflect the powerful connections they have made and the impact the literature had in supporting them as active members of the community. Increased compassion towards their peers and pride in empathetic acts among the students, is correlated to their exposure to the selected literature. Additionally, a reduction in the amount of referrals for incidents of bullying from students, teachers, and parents to the school counselor and administration is also correlated with the engagement of the literature.

Our book club provides an opportunity for the children to take their isolated thoughts into a safe environment to discuss personal experiences and bridge connections to the literature. The sharing of the book and culmination of activities in a public space reveals to the children those who may have similar experiences, allowing for them to no longer feel alone. It provides an opportunity to consider the vast experiences of others, question norms, and support or try to begin to understand them. The exposure to the critical literacy "contributes to creating spaces to take on these sorts of issues, engaging learners in powerful and pleasurable ways...to achieve a better life for all" (Vasquez, 2019, p. 308). These actions add to the sense of a community of citizens (Greene, 1995) where the entire school community is vested in these experiences and utilizes the selected literature as a conduit to understanding.

We wish for a society where, although our experiences may not be relatable, they are understandable, and in turn respected.

Selected Bibliography and Paired Activities

Throughout the course of the book club history, we have shared over fifty books with our school community. In addition to the books already discussed in this chapter, Table 1 highlights nine texts and the accompanying activities.

Table 1. Book and Activity Guide

Book Title	Activity/Music Selection
Brown, M. (2011). *Marisol McDonald doesn't match.* Children's Book Press.	The dual language story was read aloud during the assembly in both English and Spanish. Students and staff were encouraged to dress in mismatched clothing. The song True Colors (Steinberg & Kelly, 1986) was taught in advance by the music teacher and sung at the conclusion of the assembly.
De la Peña, M. (2015). *Last stop on market street.* Penguin.	A food drive was organized to collect non-perishable food items in connection to the family in the story volunteering at the soup kitchen. Upper grade students responded to the writing prompt: Who is a special person in your life? How have they helped you? What is beautiful? How do you define beauty?

Book Title	Activity/Music Selection
Hoose, P. M., Hoose, H., & Tilley, D. (1998). *Hey, little ant.* Berkley, CA: Tricycle Press.	In response to the story's ending, teachers were asked to take a vote in their classrooms – Who would squish the ant and who would let the ant be? A writing and drawing response of "What would you do at the end of the story?" was sent home. The results of the vote and selected comments from the students as to why they voted the way they did were shared during the assembly. The music teacher taught the children the song that accompanies the book which was sung at the conclusion of the assembly.
Medina, M. (2015). *Mango, Abuela, and me.* Candlewick Press (MA).	This assembly began with several teachers greeting the children in different languages (Italian, German, Greek) to provide a shared experience of what it is like to not understand when someone is speaking to you in an unknown language. Selected children, who were asked in advance if they were comfortable speaking at the assembly, shared their experience of coming to America for the first time and not speaking the same language.
Munson, D. (2000). *Enemy Pie (Reading Rainbow Book, Children's Book about Kindness, Kids Books about Learning)* (Vol. 144). Chronicle Books.	Classes met with their reading buddies to create a "friendship pie". The buddies collaboratively created a recipe for friendship. Older buddies wrote the recipe on an index card, while the younger buddies illustrated what the pie would look like on a paper plate. Completed plates and recipes were displayed in classrooms and school hallways.
Napoli, D. J. (2010). *Mama Miti: Wangari Maathai and the Trees of Kenya.* Simon and Schuster.	The video "Wangari Maathai – Planting trees IS planting hope" (https://youtu.be/XNkD hNRKYic) was shared. A "tree" was created on the main hallway bulletin board with leaves completed by each student and staff member, with a pledge of what they could do to support the environment. The family letter that was sent home provided a suggested list of activities related to Arbor Day. The song The World Is A Rainbow (Scelsa & Millang,1978) was taught by the music teacher and sung at the conclusion of the assembly.

Book Title	Activity/Music Selection
Thompson, L. A. (2015). *Emmanuel's dream: The true story of Emmanuel Ofosu Yeboah*. Schwartz & Wade.	The video "An Update on Emmanuel Ofosu Yeboah | SuperSoul Sunday | Oprah Winfrey Network" (https://www.youtube.com/watch?v=WhvS vPqISIE&t=56s) was shared. Families were invited to make a donation to L.I. Special Olympics in honor of Emmanuel Ofosu Yeboah. The song Roar (Perry et al., 2013) was taught in advance by the music teacher and sung at the conclusion of the assembly. A slide show with the lyrics and photographic images of Emmanuel was projected during the singing of the song. Children were encouraged to wear their favorite sport jersey/t-shirt to school on the day of the assembly.
Whitcomb, M. (1998). *Odd velvet*. Chronicle Books.	A Bumper Sticker (Laminack & Wadsworth, 2012) bulletin board was created where students were prompted to create supportive messages. Sharing and caring certificates were sent home with a prompt for a parent or family member to share about a time they were unkind or were treated unkindly. Students were given the opportunity to share this dialogue during their morning meeting in class.
Woodson, J. (2012). *Each kindness*. Nancy Paulsen Books.	A bulletin board of a giant sun was created in the main lobby of the school composed of individual hands created by each student and staff member. Each hand contained an illustration or description of a time they were kind to someone or someone was kind to them.

Additional Recommended Children's Literature

Boelts, M. (2007). *Those shoes*. Candlewick Press

Choi, Y. (2003). *The name jar*. Dragonfly Books.

Golenberg, P. (1992). *Teammates*. HMH Books for Young Readers.

Kostecki-Shaw, J. S. (2011). *Same, same but different*. Henry Holt and Company.

McCloud, C. (2006) *Have you filled a bucket today?: A guide to daily happiness for kids.* Ferne Press

Ludwig, T. (2013). *The invisible boy*. Knopf Books for Young Readers.

Pinkwater, D. M., & Pinkwater, M. (1977). *The big orange splot*. Scholastic.

Say, A. (2008). *Grandfather's journey*. Sandpiper.

Stead, P. C. (2010). *A sick day for Amos McGee*. Roaring Brook Press
Zemach, M. (1990). *It could always be worse: A Yiddish folktale*. Square Fish.

Appendices

Appendix A

Dear Families,

The students and staff met for the first school-wide book assembly of the school year. The book shared was *Be Kind* by Pat Zietlow Miller. This book was chosen in relation to our 2019–2020 school theme "Be Mindful". The book assembly coincided with last week's district-wide celebration of Unity Day, promoting a culture of kindness and embracing diversity. One of our teachers read the book aloud as it was projected on a large screen in the cafetorium.

Be Kind is a heartwarming story that shares the powerful message that even small acts of kindness can make a difference. In the language of the child's thoughts, the author provides examples of kindness and acknowledges that it is not always easy to be kind, especially when others aren't.

Each classroom has been provided with a copy of *Be Kind*. Additional copies are available in the school library. Children who wish to share this story at home with their families are encouraged to borrow the book from the school library.

All students decorated *kindness banners* for display in their classrooms or school hallways. Some of these banners were shared at today's assembly.

School families are encouraged to continue the discussion of kindness at home and discuss *empathy*. Here are some questions you may like to ask your child(ren) to prompt discussion:

- Have you ever seen someone who was sad and found yourself feeling sad in return?
- If you see a classmate having a rough time, what can you do to help them feel better?
- How important is it to be kind to other children, even if you don't know them?

We hope this story selection provides an opening for discussing the value and power of kindness, and ways to be kind to others.

Sincerely,

Principal _____

Appendix B

Dear Families,

The school staff understands the importance of the Dignity For All Students Act, addressing the culture of kindness and supporting the theme of embracing diversity. This year, we have continued the tradition of embracing our theme by sharing picture books that promote those ideals.

Our second book is Sparkle Boy by Leslea Newman. This story of common sibling interaction, where the younger child wants what the older child has, introduces us to Jessie whose younger brother Casey loves to play with his blocks, puzzles, and dump truck, but who also loves things that sparkle, shimmer, and glitter, like Jessie has. While the adults in Casey's life embrace his interests, Jessie isn't so sure. This is a sweet, heartwarming story about acceptance, respect, and the freedom to be you. Sparkly things are for everyone to enjoy!

This book will be shared at our next book assembly. We are inviting all of our students to wear the sparkly things that they enjoy on that day.

Each classroom is provided with a copy of the book that is shared at the book assembly. Additionally, copies are available in the school library. Children who wish to share this story at home with their families are encouraged to borrow the book from the school library.

If we hope to have young people recognize the humanity in others, it is necessary to be well rounded in these essential understandings. Families are encouraged to support our initiative. We look forward to continuing to work together, fostering a positive and safe environment for all of our children.

Sincerely,
Principal _____

Discussion Questions

1. How could you introduce the concept of a school-wide book club in your current teaching space?
2. How would you determine which themes are important to consider when selecting books for a school-wide book club?

References

Bishop, R. S. (1990). Mirrors, windows, and sliding glass doors. *Perspectives*, *6*(3), ix–xi.

Byers, G. (2018). *I am enough*. Balzer + Bray.

Freire, P. (2009). *Pedagogy of the oppressed*. Continuum. (Original work published 1970)

Greene, M. (1995). *Releasing the imagination: Essays on education, the arts, and social change*. Jossey-Bass.

Hall, M. (2015). *Red: A Crayon's story*. Greenwillow Books.

Hartman, P. (2018). A queer approach to addressing gender and sexuality through literature discussions with second graders. *Language Arts*, *96*(2), 79–90.

Laminack, L. L., & Kelly, K. (2019). *Reading to make a difference: Using literature to help students speak freely, think deeply, and take action*. Heinemann.

Laminack, L. L., & Wadsworth, R. M. (2012). *Bullying hurts: Teaching kindness through read alouds and guided conversations*. Heinemann.

Learning for Justice. (2018). *Best practices for serving LGBTQ students: A Learning for Justice guide*. Southern Poverty Law Center.

Leland, C., Harste, J., Ociepka, A., Lewison, M., & Vasquez, V. (1999). Talking about books: Exploring critical literacy: You can hear a pin drop. *Language Arts*, *77*(1), 70–77.

Luke, A. (2012). Critical literacy: Foundational notes. *Theory into practice*, *51*(1), 4–11.

Mantchev, L. (2015). *Strictly no elephants*. Simon & Schuster.

Möller, K. J. (2020). Reading and responding to LGBTQ-inclusive children's literature in school settings: Considering the state of research on inclusion. *Language Arts*, *97*(4), 235–251.

Newman, L. (2017). *Sparkle boy*. Lee and Low Books, Inc.

Nutt, A. E. (2016). *Becoming Nicole: The transformation of an American Family*. Random House.

Payne, E. C., & Smith, M. (2011). The reduction of stigma in schools: A new professional development model for empowering educators to support LGBTQ students. *Journal of LGBT Youth*, *8*(2), 174–200.

Percival, T. (2017). *Perfectly Norman*. Bloomsbury Children's Books.

Rands, K. E. (2009). Considering transgender people in education: A gender-complex approach. *Journal of Teacher Education*, *60*(4), 419–431.

Rice, P. S. (2002). Creating spaces for boys and girls to expand their definitions of masculinity and femininity through children's literature. *Journal of Children's Literature*, *28*(2), 33–42.

Ryan, C. L., Patraw, J. M., & Bednar, M. (2013). Discussing princess boys and pregnant men: Teaching about gender diversity and transgender experiences within an elementary school curriculum. *Journal of LGBT Youth*, *10*(1–2), 83–105.

Staley, S., & Leonardi, B. (2019). Complicating what we know: Focusing on educators' processes of becoming gender and sexual diversity inclusive. *Theory Into Practice*, *58*(1), 29–38.

Stock, P. L. (1995). *The dialogic curriculum: Teaching and learning in a multicultural society.* Boynton/Cook Pub.

Vasquez, V. (2007). Using the everyday to engage in critical literacy with young children. *New England Reading Association Journal, 43*(2), 6–11.

Vasquez, V., Janks, H., & Comber, B. (2019). Critical literacy as a way of being and doing. *Language Arts, 96*(5), 300–311.

Wenzel, B. (2016). *They all saw a cat.* Chronicle Books.

Zietlow Miller, P. (2018). *Be kind.* Roaring Brook Press.

Zietlow Miller, P. (2019). *When you are brave.* Little, Brown Books for Young Readers.

4. *Disability and Ableism in Literature*

JENNIFER ASHTON, GRACE KELLY & AMANDA FLUGEL

We presume that students do not notice differences and that differences do not matter. However, the opposite is true. Humans notice differences, it is the meaning that we attribute to these differences that has the potential to do great harm or provide important validation. However, we can also inflict damage by erasing or invalidating people's lived experiences. As Matthew and Clow (2007) observed, "what could possibly be worse for a child than not being included, being ignored, having your very existence denied?" (p. 72). This chapter discusses the roots of ableism in young adult and children's literature and proposes that thoughtfully chosen titles can spark conversations that challenge students to rethink their understandings of disability and disabled people. This chapter also includes a rubric, created by the authors, which teachers can use to evaluate literature for inclusion in their classroom libraries. Through intentional efforts to discuss ableism educators can prepare their students to better understand themselves and others while also helping to disrupt dominant ideologies that marginalize people.

As a source of rich narratives and counter-narratives, literature has the potential to reproduce or disrupt problematic preconceptions about various groups of people from all aspects of society. The way characters are portrayed can have a very powerful influence on readers and affect the way they perceive themselves and their relationships with others- particularly those whose identities differ from their own. This means, however, that we must rely on authors to depict characters in ways that are not only accurate, but more importantly unbiased. Problematic representations of identities perpetuate stereotypes, prejudice, and bias and reproduce inequity in society. Disability is one identity that has historically been underrepresented and misrepresented in young adult and children's literature. Unfortunately, classic young adult and children's literature is rooted in an ideology that reinforces the objectification of disabled people and reveals the depth of ableism in our social structure.

Positionality Statement

Amanda Flugel, Grace Kelly, and Dr. Jennifer Ashton are three able-bodied, cis-gender, White women. As disability scholars and educators of disabled students, we have *some* understanding of disability however, we do not identify as disabled and cannot fully understand the lived experiences of disabled people. Additionally, in recognition of the fact that many people view disability as an integral part of their identity and wish to foreground it (Davis, 2018), we have made a conscious decision to use identity-first language throughout this chapter. Any instances of person-first language occur in direct quotes as the intended words of the author.

Theoretical Framework

Traditional Special Education

The American education system has a history of marginalizing students who fall outside of the categories that have been traditionally deemed to be "normal"- White, male, heterosexual, cisgender, Christian, and non-disabled (Slesaransky-Poe & Garcia, 2014). Not even guaranteed an appropriate education until the Education for All Handicapped Children Act of 1975 was legislated, disabled students have long been an afterthought in the development of pedagogy, curriculum, and social structures in schools (Lawrence-Brown, 2014). The traditional model of special education is built on a medical model of disability (Valle & Connor, 2020) in which students who have perceived deficiencies are assessed to determine if they fit one (or more) of the definitions of the 13 classifications of disability that are tightly scripted in the Individuals with Disabilities Education Improvement Act of 2004 (the most current iteration of the original 1975 legislation) (Individuals with Disabilities Education Improvement Act [IDEIA], 2004). In a direct parallel of the medical field, once students are found eligible, they are diagnosed with a disability and then prescribed an annual Individualized Education Program (IEP) that lists their perceived deficits (and hopefully strengths) and the remedial measures that will be taken to address those deficiencies (Valle & Connor, 2020).

In this traditional model of special education, professionals look into the body/mind of the student to find out what is wrong with them (according to currently accepted socio-cultural-educational standards of normalcy) and seek ways to fix or cure the students so that they can be returned to "normal" classification. In this structure, disabled students often spend up to 13 years in a system that indexes them as deviant and deficient and not worthy of full membership in general education classes and schools. Assumptions are made about students' intellectual capabilities, literacy, desires, needs, and strengths based on widely accepted, but socially constructed, standards of normalcy. These assumptions often start with a deficit view of the student and presume a basic incompetence and inability to learn and grow like their non-disabled peers (Biklen & Burke, 2006).

Disability Studies in Education

Disability Studies in Education (DSE) is a critical theoretical perspective that not only challenges the medical model of traditional special education, but also provides an alternate social model of disability that not only recognizes, but begins with the wholeness of disabled people. Rather than situating the 'problem' within the body/mind of the disabled student, DSE recognizes a wide range of 'normalness' in humanity and puts the onus of change on schools, administrators, and teachers to meet the needs of disabled students in inclusive educational settings (Ashby, 2012; Baglieri & Shapiro, 2017; Ware, 2001). DSE provides us with a perspective and language with which we can counter long-dominant grand narratives that situate some students on the deficient side of the normal/abnormal binary.

This socially constructed (and historically shifting) normal/abnormal binary has permeated education systems for over one hundred years and has resulted in a separate but unequal dual system of education in which general education (normal) students receive an education that prepares them for meaningful post-school life. While, special education (abnormal) students often receive a substandard education that leaves them more likely to be undereducated, unprepared for higher education, unemployed and incarcerated (Slesaransky-Poe & Garcia, 2014; Valle & Connor, 2020). Disabled students are routinely placed in segregated classrooms or schools solely for disabled students, while the more fortunate ones are placed in nominally inclusive general education classrooms but removed to receive their special education services (treatment). Further complicating the impact and consequences of special education, we know that students of color are much more likely than their White peers to be classified as disabled in school because of systemic racism and a lack of cultural understanding or empathy in a predominantly white teaching force (Garguilo & Bouck, 2021; Slesaransky-Poe &

Garcia, 2014). This overrepresentation has persisted for decades and makes it even more difficult for students of color to be successful in school.

The key factor to consider here is that disability is deemed to be undesirable, in need of treatment, and best handled out of the public eye. Through federal legislation that allows for segregated education, many disabled students are subject to a substandard curriculum and their civil rights are routinely oppressed by the very system that seeks to help them. The name for this type of oppression is *ableism*. "Similar to other systems of oppressions, such as racism, sexism, classism, and heterosexism, ableism thrives on beliefs about the inherent superiority of some and the inferiority of others on the basis of group traits" (Baglieri & Lalvani, 2020, p. 2). With the rationalization of ableism so deeply ingrained in the grand narrative of disability, most non-disabled people (and some disabled people) do not even recognize this type of oppression and tacitly accept it as reasonable.

Intersectionality

Not without criticism, though, the field of Disability Studies has been overwhelmingly dominated by White voices and experiences. Disability rights scholar, Christopher Bell, refers to this as "White Disability Studies." Bell (2016) explains the varying ways in which Black and brown people are continually silenced and ignored in Disability Studies. Along similar lines, disability activist, Vilissa Thompson, created the social media movement #DisabilityTooWhite (Leary, 2017), bringing attention to the erasure of Black and brown people from Disability Studies and activism. With the overrepresentation of students of color in special education and the predominance of White perspectives in scholarship, it is clear that students' experiences in special education may vary greatly because of other identities that they may have.

Disability is an identity that one can have alongside many identities including, but not limited to, race, gender, class, ethnicity, sexuality, and religion (Beverley, 2009; Thomson, 1997). Crenshaw (1989), introduced the term intersectionality, which emphasizes how an individual's multiple identities are interrelated and construct their social, political, educational, and cultural experiences. Using this lens, it is important for educators to also consider how their students' many identities intersect, and how those intersections might impact their students' lives.

Building on Crenshaw's work with intersectionality, DisCrit, a recently emerged critical framework, seeks to expose the ways in which race and ability are so deeply interrelated in social and cultural conceptions of normalcy. DisCrit, asserts that "racism and ableism often work in ways that are unspoken, yet racism validates and reinforces ableism, and ableism validates and reinforces racism" (Annamma et al., 2016, p. 14). Erevelles (2018) explains that, "When racism intersects with ableism, the lives of disabled people of color are placed in double jeopardy" (p. 119). Literature that stigmatizes or erases race and disability only fuels the sense of alienation that many people with non-dominant identities experience and reinforces problematic constructions of normalcy.

Representation in Literature

Problematic Representation of Disabilities

As discussed in the previous section, disabled students are often excluded from daily activities and learning in the classroom. Similarly, disabled characters are not often seen in books and if they are, they typically do not represent real lives and experiences of disabled people. Young adult and children's texts have the potential to create space for transformation in peoples' attitudes about disability, but they also risk reproducing problematic stereotypes (Adomat, 2014). If young adult and children's literature portrays disability at all, it is typically marked by "negative portrayals, misconceptions, and stereotypes of disability" (Ware, 2018, p. 263). These texts often depict disabled characters as "the mean deformed person, the evil villain, or the odd, childlike person" (Baglieri & Lalvani, 2020, p. 137). From Captain Hook to Quasimodo, students are shown narratives that showcase disability as something that needs to be feared, cured, eliminated, or overcome and that a life with a disability is isolating and tragic (Baglieri & Lalvani, 2020; Matthew & Clow, 2016; Perry & Carter-Long, 2018). In order to make sure that teachers are not unintentionally reproducing the harmful effects of ableism in literature, they must carefully select books that depict disabled characters in non-biased ways.

Representation of Intersectionality

It is not enough to simply include disabled voices, stories, and experiences in classroom curriculum. Curriculum and texts included should be representative of differing identities and experiences, ensuring that intersectionality is acknowledged. Educators must provide students with the opportunity to learn about other identities that they may not possess and how those identities intersect to impact another person's life. Carefully and thoughtfully chosen literature that presents positive representations of multiple identities is essential for this, but it is often challenging to find as literature often reinforces dominant ideology and stereotypical identities.

Many of the characters in young adult and children's literature are "overwhelmingly White, predominantly upper middle class, heterosexual, nondisabled, English-speaking, and male" (Crisp et al., 2016, p. 29) and individuals with marginalized identities are often excluded. However, in young adult and children's literature it is common for books about marginalized characters to be written by authors who do not share the same marginalized identities (Duyvis, 2015). While this may be done with good intentions, the depictions of characters are often misleading, offensive or damaging. The texts that are readily available to students communicate what their school, community and world value and the dearth of representative texts presents a challenge for many students with non-dominant identities (Johnson & Koss, 2016). With the dominance of non-disabled White authors in young adult and children's literature, it is difficult to locate texts written by Black and brown disabled authors about Black and brown disabled children. As a result, students may receive the message that Black and brown disabled stories are not worthy or important, which makes the careful and intentional selection of texts even more important for educators.

The literature that we share with our students should have characters with complex identities. In books where there are disabled characters, disability should be portrayed as just one of the many identities, and not the central focus of the text. Additionally, books with disabled characters should not seek to educate people about a specific disability. When disability is included, it is often positioned in a way where the intention is to educate about a particular disability, rather than a text where a character's complex identity includes disability among other traits (Beverley, 2009). "Characters with disabilities are increasingly more complex with story lines and relationships that include, but also extend beyond disability" (Baglieri & Lalvani, 2020, p. 156). Young adult and children's literature should portray characters as complete humans regardless of their disability status.

Importance in Book Choice

For many children, their first exposure to literature occurs when they enter the education system. Literature provides children with mirrors and windows (Bishop, 1990). Ideally, a balance between these types of texts is what educators should inspire to have in their classroom libraries. Children from dominant social groups are frequently able to see themselves reflected in the texts they read. These mirror texts contribute to the reproduction of dominant conceptions of normalcy. With fewer opportunities to read mirror texts, children from marginalized social groups often experience texts as windows.

The realities of these window texts may be starkly different from students' own lived experiences, leaving them feeling devalued in the classroom community (Bishop, 1990).

Through thoughtful selection of texts, educators can provide disabled students with mirrors, where they can see their value in the classroom and global community (Bishop, 2015). It is equally important for their nondisabled peers to read window texts that center disabled characters and their personal stories. Research indicates that "children's attitudes towards individuals with disabilities can be influenced by the way characters with disabilities are depicted in literature" (Wilkins et al., 2016, p. 236). As educators we should be exposing our students to mirror and window literature that has the potential to affirm their identities and broaden their understanding of humanity.

Acknowledging that book selection can be daunting when one needs to consider the many identities and perspectives that should be represented, we have created a rubric (Table 1) to assist educators with this work. This rubric consists of five broad themes and a series of related guiding questions for educators to consider when selecting texts to use in their classrooms and instruction. In using the rubric, the responses to the guiding questions will indicate potential problematic areas as well as the overall appropriateness of the text. While we understand that few texts will meet all of the expectations in the rubric, ideally, we would like to have as many "yes" responses as possible to ensure the appropriateness of the text.

Table 1. Rubric to select texts related to Disability and Ableism

Theme	Guiding Questions	Yes	No
Author(s): *It is important to consider the author of the text. The creators of the text are just as important as the purpose behind the text. The authors influence the information that is depicted within texts. For example, non-disabled authors, teachers, parents of disabled students, and disabled people will all have different perspectives. Own-voices texts are preferred.*	Can you confirm that the author is portraying disability authentically and accurately? Is this an Own-Voices text?		

Theme	Guiding Questions	Yes	No
Portrayal of disability: *Disabled people should be portrayed as active participants in family, school, work, and/or community contexts. Disabled students should not be portrayed as objects of curiosity, sensationalized, or endowed with superhuman attributes.*	Is the disabled person a protagonist or narrator in the text? Are disabled people shown in a variety of physical settings? Is disability portrayed as a caricature or in a way that perpetuates stereotypes? Does the text enable readers to witness multiple dimensions of disabled people's lives?		
Ableism: *Disabled characters should be portrayed alongside non-disabled characters in non-biased and equitable ways.*	Does the text challenge able-bodied students to consider their privilege? Does the text name ableism?		
Intersectionality: *Characters should be presented as whole complex beings possessing multiple identities. Texts should depict more than one person's experience in order to illustrate a variety of experiences related to disability. The narrative should provide enough information to consider age, race, gender, and other contextual factors as influencing elements of the perspectives depicted.*	Does the text enable understanding that disability is a diverse identity? Does the text construct characters as whole complex beings with multiple identities? Does the text acknowledge that the characters' experiences are not representative of all experiences of disabled individuals?		
The take-away: *Stories should not have "happily ever after" plots that situate the student's disability as an obstacle in need of overcoming. We should always remember that disabled students have aspirations just like their non-disabled peers (social model of disability).*	Does the text problematize eradicating or curing disability and instead promote acceptance and wholeness? Does the text demonstrate that disability is a natural part of life and that life with disabilities, like other lives, has ups and downs, challenges, and joys? Are disabled people shown interacting with others in reciprocal relationships as valuable members of their communities?		

Adapted from Baglieri and Lalvani (2020), Undoing ableism: Teaching about disability in K-12 classrooms, Routledge

Adapted from Matthew and Clow (2007), Putting disabled children in the picture: Promoting inclusive children's books and media. *International Journal of Early Childhood, 39(2), 65–72*

Discussion About Books and Authors

#OwnVoices

Disabled people are largely invisible in children's literature- this includes not only characters, but also the writers and illustrators of the stories (Matthew & Clow, 2016). No one knows the complexities, oppression, or lived experiences of someone with a disability better than a person who is disabled themselves. A social media movement began in 2015 to recognize and widely share texts centering marginalized characters written by authors who share the same marginalized identity. Duyvis (2015) created #OwnVoices on Twitter, to amplify these stories and authors. Duyvis identifies as a queer disabled person and has authored many well-developed stories that center disabled characters. The #OwnVoices movement is a great resource and helpful reminder that as educators we should be centering marginalized voices, and disrupting systems of inequity in our classrooms. Additionally, Duyvis maintains the website "Disability in Kidlit" as a resource for educators who are looking for texts written by marginalized authors about marginalized characters.

Book Disclaimer

The books described here represent many of the positive aspects that we have discussed in this chapter. However, it is important to note that finding books written by disabled authors was a challenge, and this list of books is not intended to be exhaustive or ideal. In order to provide a selection of books that can be used at any level, we have arranged the books in the two following sections in ascending order from lower to higher reading levels. We resist categorizing the books any further to make the point that having high interest/low readability text options is essential to meet the needs of some students who might still be developing the necessary skills to read at what many consider to be an age-appropriate level.

Children's Book Choices

One fun illustrated children's book is *Armond Goes to a Party: A book about Aspergers and Friendship* by Nancy Carlson & Armond Isaak. It is important to acknowledge that although Aspergers is no longer recognized as a diagnosis, it is now part of a broader category of Autism Spectrum Disorder. Despite this, we feel that the value of this book is in the story that is shared and not the label. An own-voices text, this book is based on one of the co-authors, Armond Isaak's, life. When Armond was diagnosed with autism, he couldn't find any books that he could connect to and began to feel lonely and isolated.

- As the protagonist of the story, Armond is an active participant in his family, with his friends, and in his community.
- The book enables readers to witness multiple dimensions of Armond's life as he attends his friend's birthday party where simple accommodations were made to support his needs.
- The text demonstrates that disability is a natural part of life and that life with disabilities, like other lives, has ups and downs, challenges, and joys.
- The children's book discusses how different people have different needs and how we can help others feel included.

Charlotte and the Quiet Place by Deborah Sosin is a children's book based in a colorful and noisy bustling city. Charlotte, a young disabled Black girl living in New York City, finds loud noises to be quite troublesome and overwhelming.

- Unlike previous children's books mentioned, this is not an own-voices text. The author Deborah Sosin is an able-bodied white woman. However, this text portrays the protagonist, Charlotte, as a whole complex being with multiple intersecting identities.
- The text shows how Charlotte manages her reactions to the sounds that trouble her and is able to be an active participant in family, school, and her community.
- This text promotes acceptance and wholeness.

A Boy and a Jaguar is an own-voices text where author Alan Rabinowitz recounts his struggles with stuttering throughout his childhood. He is a student, a scholar, and an advocate for leopards. As a child he went to the zoo and saw a sad, caged jaguar and he promised he would be a voice for the animals. Feeling a kinship with the jaguars, Alan's stutter disappeared when he spoke to the animals. The connection that he felt to them continued throughout his life as he has used his voice to advocate for big cats around the world.

- This book shows the disabled protagonist in a variety of physical settings across his lifetime.
- Alan is a valuable member of the community with strong relationships.
- As Alan grows up, his stutter is just one of his many identities.

Young Adult Book Choices

Emma-Jean Lazarus Fell Out of a Tree by Lauren Tarishis is written about middle-schooler, Emma, who uses logic to guide all of her social interactions. Her thinking and mannerisms are similar to that of her late father, a mathematician and logical thinker. Emma, the protagonist, is not interested in becoming friends with her fellow seventh grader peers, as their emotions are always running wild. However, when Emma sees her peer, Colleen, crying in the bathroom she wonders if she can use her logical thinking to help.

- The text demonstrates that although Emma's social mannerisms may be different, she is capable of reciprocal relationships with her peers.
- While this text is not an own-voices text, Lauren Tarishis disclosed that she has a learning disability, which made it difficult for her to learn to read.
- In her writing Tarishis does not propose that Emma needs to be "fixed" in order to develop reciprocal relationships, but rather her unique social skills make Emma's relationships thrive.

Ride High Pineapple, an own-voices text by Jenny Woolsey, follows the life of thirteen-year old Isabelle Burgess as she navigates school, crushes, friendships, and anxiety. Unlike the rest of her school age peers, Issy has Crouzon, a craniofacial syndrome.

- Similar to Issy, author Jenny Woolsey, and her two children share the same disability as Issy.
- This text positions Issy as a complex being with multiple intersecting identities.
- Importantly, Issy is depicted as capable of reciprocal relationships with friends, and family.
- Like most middle and high-schoolers the text demonstrates that Issy is capable of crushes and adolescent romantic relationships.
- *Ride High Pineapple* is an important own-voices text that shows how disabled teens, like most teens, are simply trying to make it through adolescence.

Founder of #OwnVoices movement, Corinne Duyvis, wrote the young adult book *On the Edge of Gone*. This text is narrated by protagonist Denise, as her and her family prepare for an apocalyptic comet to hit Earth. They are lucky to find a ship leaving before the comet strikes, the only problem is that each passenger must have a practical skill in order to board. Denise is autistic and worries her disability will bar her from fleeing to safety.

- The text emphasizes intersectionality, as characters are crafted with complex and unique identities.
- Duyvis uses her own experiences with disability to bring Denise's character to life during a thrilling apocalypse. Duyvis' identities as queer and autistic relate to multiple characters in the book.
- The text is not focused on how to cure autism or diagnose it, but rather Denise's autism is just one of many factors that may impact her ability to board the ship.

Conclusion

According to Baglieri and Lalvani (2020), "the marginalization of and discrimination against people on the basis of having uncommon and unusual bodies and minds has occurred throughout time and place" (p. 183). As inclusive educators, we must disrupt practices that contribute to the erasure of disability and challenge ourselves, our administrators, and our students to think more broadly about ableism, normalcy, and difference. With that in mind, educators should be thinking about ways in which they can cultivate a classroom library with rich and diverse characters, stories and authors. We acknowledge that it is important to build representative classroom libraries, but that alone is insufficient. The *Rubric to Select Texts Related to Disability and Ableism* provides a framework with which educators can evaluate texts for use in their classrooms. The questions posed in this rubric illuminate many potentially problematic aspects of literature and are intended to spark further critical thought and conversation about disability, representation, and ableism. It is our hope that using this rubric will cultivate opportunities for reciprocal learning experiences among and between educators and students. It is easy to become overwhelmed with current events that highlight the injustices and inequities experienced by so many people in our society leaving us feeling powerless to effect any meaningful change. With this chapter, we hope to provide you with a tool that you can use to reassign meaning to disability and disrupt ableist beliefs and practices in your school communities.

Discussion Questions

1. Using the rubric provided, evaluate a book you plan to use in your classroom. What did you notice about the book based on your evaluation? Does the information from the rubric confirm your decision to use the book?

References

Adomat, D. (2014). Exploring issues of disability in children's literature discussion. *Disability Studies Quarterly, 34*(3). https://doi.org/10.18061/dsq.v34i3.3865

Annamma, S. A., Connor, D. J., & Ferri, B. A. (2016). Dis/ability critical race studies (DisCrit): Theorizing at the intersections of race and dis/ability. In D. J. Connor, B. A. Ferri, & S. A. Annamma (Eds.), *DisCrit: Disability studies and critical race theory in education* (pp. 9–32). Teachers College Press.

Ashby, C. (2012). Disability studies and inclusive teacher preparation: A socially just path for teacher education. *Research & Practice for Persons with Severe Disabilities, 37*(2), 89–99. https://doi-org.brockport.idm.oclc.org/10.2511/027494812802573611

Baglieri, S., & Lalvani, P. (2020). *Undoing ableism: Teaching about disability in K-12 classrooms.* Routledge.

Baglieri, S., & Shapiro, A. (2017). *Disability Studies and the inclusive classroom* (2nd ed.). Routledge.

Bell, C. (2006). Introducing white disability studies: A modest proposal. In L. Davis (Ed.), *The disability studies reader* (2nd ed., pp. 275–282). Routledge.

Beverley, B. (2009). Creating characters with diversity in mind: Two Canadian authors discuss social constructs of disability in literature for children. *Language and Literacy, 11*(1), 1–19. https://doi.org/10.20360/G2201G

Biklen, D., & Burke, J. (2006). Presuming competence. *Equity and Excellence in Education, 39*(2), 166–175. https://doi.org/10.1080/10665680500540376

Bishop, R. S. (1990). Mirror, windows, and sliding glass doors. *Perspectives: Choosing and using books for the classrooms, 6*(3). ix–xi

Crenshaw, K. (1989). Demarginalizing the intersection of race and sex: A black feminist critique of antidiscrimination doctrine, feminist theory and antiracist politics. *University of Chicago Legal Forum, 1989*(1), 139–167.

Crisp, T., Knezek, S. M., Quinn, M., Bingham, G. E., Girardeau, K., & Starks, F. (2016). What's on our bookshelves? The diversity of children's literature in early childhood classroom libraries. *Journal of Children's Literature, 42*(2), 29–42.

Davis, L. (2018). Introduction. In L. Davis (Ed.), *Beginning with disability: A primer.* Routledge.

Duyvis, C. (2015). *#Ownvoices frequently asked questions.* Corinne Duyvis Sci-Fi & Fantasy in MG & YA. http://www.corinneduyvis.net/ownvoices/

Education for All Handicapped Children Act of 1975. Pub. Law No. 94-142.

Erevelles, N. (2018). Disability and race. In L. Davis (Ed.), *Beginning with disability a primer* (pp. 115–122). Routledge.

Gargiulo, R. & Bouk, E. (2021). *Special Education in Contemporary Society.* Sage.

Individuals with Disabilities Education Act, 20 U.S.C. § 1400 (2004).

Johnson, D. & Koss, M. (2016). Diversity in children's literature: 1 year later. *Journal of Children's Literature, 42*(1), 53–56.

Lawrence-Brown, D. (2014). Understanding critical perspectives: Who benefits? In Lawrence-Brown & Sapon-Shevin (Eds.), *Condition critical: Key principles for equitable and inclusive education.* Teachers College Press.

Leary, A. (2017, June 14). Reflecting on the impact of #disabilitytoowhite. *Rooted in Rights* https://rootedinrights.org/reflecting-on-the-impact-of-disabilitytoowhite/

Matthew, N., & Clow, S. (2007). Putting disabled children in the picture: Promoting inclusive children's books and media. *International Journal of Early Childhood, 39*(2), 65–72.

Perry, D. M., & Carter-Long, L. (2018). How misunderstanding disability leads to police violence. In L. Davis (Ed.), *Beginning with disability a primer* (pp. 165–168). Routledge (Reprinted from "How misunderstanding disability leads to police violence," by D. M. Perry & L. Carter-Long, 2014, *The Atlantic.*).

Slesaransky-Poe, G., & Garcia, A. M. (2014). The social construction of difference. In Lawrence-Brown & Sapon-Shevin (Eds.), *Condition critical: Key principles for equitable and inclusive education.* Teachers College Press.

Thomson, R. G. (1997). *Extraordinary bodies: Figuring physical disability in American culture and literature.* Columbia University Press.

Valle, J. W., & Connor, D. J. (2011). *Rethinking disability: A disability studies approach to inclusive practices.* McGraw-Hill.

Ware, L. (2001). Writing, identity, and the other: Dare we do disability studies? *Journal of Teacher Education, 52*(2), 107–123.

Ware, L. (2018). Disability studies in k-12 education. In L. Davis (Ed.), *Beginning with disability a primer* (pp. 259–268). Routledge

Wilkins, J., Howe, K., Seiloff, M., Rowan, S., & Lilly, E. (2016). Exploring elementary students' perceptions of disabilities using children's literature. *British Journal of Special Education, 43*(3), 233–249.

5. *Who is in Your Family?: Moving Toward a More Inclusive Representation of Diverse Families in Children's Literature*

AMY SHEMA

Can you imagine if you're a child and you don't see, you know, talk about all these different kinds of families, but yours isn't there. Then you think to yourself well, what's wrong with my family, why isn't my family shown in this book, or talked about.

This was a quote from a first grade teacher who was explaining the importance of students needing to see representations of their family in schools. Yet, sometimes the best intentions do not always translate into practice. This same teacher, when asked about the kinds of activities she taught related to students' families, showed me a large paper titled "All About Me," that had a box drawn in the center labeled "_____'s Nuclear Family". Lines connected the center box to five boxes around the perimeter of the paper, labeled, "Mom," "Dad," "Brothers," "Sisters," and "Pets." On the reverse side, the center box was labeled, "____'s Extended Family," and mirrored the same layout, but the labels in the boxes read, "Aunt," "Uncle," Grandma," "Grandpa," and "Cousins" instead. The teacher explained to me that at the beginning of the school year, she had the students draw their families on these diagrams. The diagrams were displayed around the classroom for Open House. After the teacher explained the activity to me, I asked her what happened if a student did not have a mom or dad. She told me, "They just leave it blank." I then asked, "What happens if they have two moms, like in a blended family; so you have a mom and a stepmom?" The teacher replied, "They usually just draw their biological mom" (Shema, 2015, p. 202). I asked, "What happens if they have two moms and no dad?" "They can just draw an extra box and leave the other empty", she replied. To me, this was a dismissive response that further exemplified the problem with boxes and labels, thus reinforcing those who fit inside the box, and those who do not.

I recounted this anecdote during one of my college courses on critical literacy and asked the teacher candidates what they thought of this kind of activity. One candidate shared, "It's just not right. Kids come from so many different kinds of families. What gives the teachers the right to tell kids which families are normal and which aren't?" I asked the candidate to explain. He replied, "The teachers actually created boxes where certain families fit and others do not. When these papers are displayed, all of the other kids know who has a dad, who doesn't, or who doesn't even live with their parents."

I asked if there is any benefit to having students share their family structures. Another teacher candidate said that there is benefit from sharing and that it is important for children to share about their families as well as to learn about others. What becomes problematic is the language that we as teachers use to describe families and who adults, teachers in this case, value as legitimate members of a family.

Positionality Statement

I am a white, cisgender, able-bodied woman who works at a state university. I teach in a teacher certification program and am the director of a summer enrichment program for school-age students residing in the city. My interest in representations of diverse families started when I taught first and second grade in an urban district. During that time, I had difficulty locating texts with characters who resembled my students. This conspicuous absence of people of color in texts became complicated when taking into account the family relationships between adults and children. Many of my students would share stories about primary care-givers other than their biological mothers or fathers. I noticed that some colleagues would talk from a deficit mindset about children having absent fathers or children being raised by grandparents. However, I was excited to celebrate all of those family members who love and care for my students. Yet most children's books included White characters with heterosexual parents living in one household, which did not reflect my students' lives. It is not my intent to vilify the aforementioned family constellation, rather to shed light on the need for diverse representations of families so that all children can see both models that reflect their experiences, as well as families that are different from their own.

Schools as Cultural Institutions

Schools are social spaces where children learn about their own lives and about the lives of others. Because schools are cultural institutions that influence children's identity development, children must be able to experience school as a place where their own life experiences are legitimized and valued if they are to become confident, competent citizens. They also need to witness and engage with other family models to learn about the myriad constellations of others' life experiences.

A sociocultural-historical perspective emphasizes that schools are situated among larger social institutions and learning happens through participation in particular discourse communities. Members of a discourse community use linguistic practices (reading, writing, speaking, listening) that have certain expectations, rules, and underlying assumptions to guide norms of acceptability. It is within discourse communities that children engage in social practices and learn social norms and behaviors (Barton & Hamilton, 1998; Gee, 2015). These discourses serve an important role in society, especially related to maintaining systems of privilege by appearing to be neutral or benign. It is through these hegemonic functions, or unquestioned assumed truths, that certain models are promoted as "normal" or a form of common sense (Gee, 2015). Consequently, any model that does not fit the model of "normal" is deemed to be "abnormal."

As cultural institutions, schools are not value-neutral, nor is the curriculum (Apple, 2001) and the discourses enacted in schools "support the continuation of established, powerful organizations as they constantly work to maintain their dominance" (Compton-Lilly, 2004, p. 21). Therefore, schools and curriculum are political spaces, not politics related to political parties i.e. Democrat or Republican, rather political in the sense that there are structures to maintain inequitable distributions of power grounded in hegemonic ideologies. Teaching is a political act because teachers are primary agents in a political arena. Even in a hyper-polarized political climate, the belief that teachers can be politically "neutral," is in itself a political decision. Choosing to not engage in topics for fear of entering into "controversial" territory further marginalizes those whose humanity is already being debated (Miller et al., 2020). If teachers are committed to social justice and equity, their pedagogical obligation is to ensure that what they teach and the classroom environment is responsive and affirming of all identities. When various identity groups are questioned as appropriate or not, the messages that teachers send only reinforces that honoring others as worthy of respect is optional (Miller et al., 2020).

Why Is This Important?

Sociocultural-historical theory serves as a theoretical framework for critical literacy because it emphasizes an individual's active participation in a constantly changing community of learners, in which knowledge is constructed within larger cultural systems (Barton & Hamilton, 1998; Larson & Marsh, 2015; Rogoff, 2003). This approach is in contrast to what Street (1995) refers to as "autonomous models of literacy," or a set of neutral skills that can be applied across contexts independent of the user. Whereas, sociocultural-historical theory as applied to literacy as a social practice posits that knowledge is constructed in a mutually constituted process in which learning occurs through interaction that is dynamically co-constructed (Larson & Marsh, 2015; Rogoff, 2003). According to Larson and Marsh (2015),

> Individuals and groups construct worldviews (everyday realities) in interaction with society. These constructed worldviews are mediated by language and culture in an ongoing process of identity construction. In other words, the meaning of everyday concepts such as gender and teaching are highly contingent on social, cultural, historical, and political processes. (p. 7)

Within this view, teachers and students learn what constitutes "appropriate" or "normal" behavior through the social spaces in which they operate. Those social spaces are also replete with power structures and opportunities for disruptions.

Having children's literature that includes diverse characters and families is a first step in shifting dominant narratives. How teachers talk about and engage in critical conversations with students is also important to students' identity development. Tschida and Buchanan (2017) shared teachers' experiences of feeling "uncomfortable talking about certain types of families (i.e., same-gender, multiracial, foster, homeless) for fear of offending some parents or getting in trouble with administrations" (p. 4). Yet, my research (Shema, 2015) regarding teachers' inclusion of LGBTQI-headed families in elementary curriculum demonstrated that this fear was unlikely, and teachers often used the rationale of "needing to respect parents' beliefs" as justification to avoid including non-traditional family constellations. This rhetoric privileges heteronormative families by respecting some family's values, while disrespecting others.

Ryan and Hermann-Wilmarth (2018) want teachers to ask students questions that draw attention to various identity categories and what students know, or assume, about them in order to expose stereotypes and misconceptions. They emphasize that teachers need to not only question if there is

LGBTQI representation but how they are represented, as those representations are the message to students.

It is through these critical conversations that students are not just consumers of texts, but have agency in their literacy practices.

Literacy as a Social Practice

Language is dynamic – ever changing, evolving, contextual, and cultural; it is never neutral, and it is always political (Barton & Hamilton, 1998; Gee, 2015; Shannon, 1992). Meaning is never inherent; literacy is more than words on a page, meaning is made in socially mediated context-specific interactions. Language does not exist without use, in other words, literacy is a social practice (Barton & Hamilton, 1998; Larson & Marsh, 2015).

Therefore, texts are not neutral or void of politics. Regardless of the genre, publisher, or intended use, all texts are created in socially mediated contexts and as cultural beings, all human engagement with those texts are subjective. It is through humans making meaning of text that information is co-constructed and shared. Therefore, engaging in critical literacy practices encourages readers to pose questions about the text that unpacks some of the hidden assumptions shrouded in dominant discourses. Critical literacy approaches texts as contextual works grounded in social, political, economic, historical, and identity politics. Through critical literacy practices, readers can interrogate power relations and can become more aware of their own experiences rooted in structures of privilege and marginalization (Bishop, 2014). Likewise, teaching is a political act and positions families as a specific kind of relationship between adults and children (Compton-Lilly, 2003). How those relationships are organized is also politically defined.

When literacy is approached as a social practice, or something that people "do," rather than something that people "have," engaging with texts becomes transformative because the "reader" redesigns and reconstructs meaning. It is within these spaces that power can be shifted. Vasquez, Janks, and Comber (2019) explain that "Critical literacy focuses on the interplay between discursive practices and unequal power relations – and issues of social justice and equity – in support of diverse learners" (p. 302). As such, critical literacy can be an approach for those populations who have been historically marginalized or absent from texts, to be shifted to the center.

For example, when I select a book for a child to read independently, I look for indications about who the characters are, where do they live, what are the activities they are doing, and then ask if any of those images or concepts reinforce dominant ideologies or challenge them. Are characters depicted in stereotypical clothing, roles, or activities? If so, I ask "Why?" Are these aspects of the plot that are going to be addressed or assumptions that the author has made because of normative perspectives? As the teacher, I need to ask myself, "What messages are the children going to take away after engaging with this text?" It is my goal that engaging with this text provides opportunities for critique of contemporary society by calling into question inequities, repositioning structures of power, and leading to more just systems.

Representation Matters: Mirrors and Windows

One way to interrupt the dominant discourses of schools is to ensure that children have diverse texts that encourage what Bishop (1990) refers to as being able to experience both "mirrors" into one's own and "windows" into others' life experiences. Children need to be exposed to various family constellations in texts. Seeing oneself represented in texts is validating, identity forming, and critical to development. Bishop (1990) argues that when children see themselves depicted in a positive light, those characteristics are reinforced as attributes to aspire. However, when children are absent from text, or images are stereotypes, inaccurate, or misleading, then they also learn which elements are devalued and even shunned. Similarly, seeing others' perspectives and experiences prepares students to engage with the larger diverse world (Ryan & Hermann-Wilmarth, 2018; Tschida et al., 2014). Bishop (1990) reminds us, "Children from dominant social groups have always found their mirrors in books, but they, too, have suffered from the lack of availability of books about others. They need the books as windows onto reality, not just imaginary worlds" (para. 5). Literature provides both the mirrors and windows for readers to explore people and cultures they have encountered as well as those foreign to them.

Although the average American classroom has become more diverse, the percentage of books depicting characters from diverse backgrounds has not kept up. Data on books published for children and teens by and about people of color and from First/Native Nations has been compiled by the Cooperative Children's Book Center, School of Education, University of Wisconsin-Madison (http://ccbc.education.wisc.edu/books/pcstats.asp). According to their review of books published in 2018, characters were depicted in the following percentages:

- American Indians/First Nations (1%)
- Latinx (5%)
- Asian Pacific Islander/Asian Pacific American (7%)

- African/African American (10%)
- Animals/Other (27%)
- White (50%)

These percentages have improved since the 2015 reporting of diversity in children's books in which over 73% of all children's books published that year had White characters (SLJ, 2019).

Though the heterosexual family has been normalized through texts and media, exposure to diverse family constellations, various relationships among members, and a range of adult roles, benefits all children's healthy social development. Even though families may look different, families should all function to meet the similar goals of nurturing the health and wellbeing of their members. As such, children need to not only experience a curriculum that is representative of their own families, but classroom instruction and discussions need to include and acknowledge all family structures.

When children's literature is inclusive of the diverse experiences of children and society, children are afforded the opportunity to learn about people who are already in their lives, providing validation for their own experiences. Children who engage with curriculum that mirrors their own lives feel that it helps to validate them in the public space of school. It is important for children to see themselves represented in the curriculum in order to foster confidence, improve motivation, and establish healthy peer relations. Likewise, research shows that when children do not see their family structures represented in the curriculum, there can be negative consequences on their identity development, which can lead to poor self-esteem, interpersonal struggles, and low academic performance (Casper & Schultz, 1999; Ladson-Billings, 1994).

As family structures continue to change throughout societies, as well as their roles throughout a child's life, educators need to be aware of the various ways children view their own families and who counts as family regardless of kith (choice) or kin (biological) relation. This need for family awareness is based on the research that has indicated meaningful family engagement in children's early learning can positively impact school readiness and later academic success (Weiss et al., 2006). Plus, we all have a need to belong.

Social Construction of Family

Families are one of the most fundamental units of societies and are critical in the identity development of children. Families serve an integral role in the formation of value systems and thinking patterns by being "a gateway through which children are introduced to the dominant social norms"

(Larrabee & Kim, 2010, p. 351). There are terms in dominant discourse that people use in a way that assumes a shared meaning, even when our own experiences tell us differently. The concepts of nuclear and extended family depict very specific kinds of family constellations and have defined relationships between family members. We know that children are raised in a myriad of family constellations that are as unique as the child. Family dynamics, and who is considered to be a primary care-giver, can also change over time. For children raised by grandparents, aunts, uncles, or in multiple households, the nuclear and extended family models do not apply, yet this is the model often depicted in schools and by teachers. Children are quite adept at recognizing when and where they fit into the framework of what constitutes a "normal" family.

Family models such as "nuclear" and "extended" are rooted in European traditions, and consist of a mother, father, and children as a nuclear "unit" and grandparents, aunts/uncles, and cousins as "extended" family (Surtees & Gunn, 2010). The notion of nuclear family, composed of a father, a mother, and progeny living together in one residence, is the result of intentional and unintentional promotion and enculturation, which does not mirror the way many world cultures rear their children.

Whereas, families of the African diaspora often include aunts and uncles as primary caregivers and references to cousins may not necessarily be delineated blood-related kinship. Instead, cousins may be close friends, included as family and referred to as "fictive kin" (Chatters et al., 1994). Latinx family constellations often include multiple generations residing together or in close proximity (Landale et al., 2006). Bell (2009) argues that family units in the United States have historically been defined by heterosexual marriage and serves the interests of the "state," rather than the needs of individuals. This definition serves legal purpose and privileges certain family constellations as more legitimate than others.

America's Children: Key National Indicators of Well-Being (2019) highlights several changing demographics of United States' school-age populations. Of particular note is the dramatic growth in racial and ethnic diversity among students and family constellations. From data collected in 2018, it was projected that by 2020 less than half of all children will be White, non-Hispanic, and by 2050, that percentage will decrease to 39%; where 31% will be Hispanic; 14% will be Black, non-Hispanic; 7% will be Asian, non-Hispanic; and 9% will be non-Hispanic "All other races."

Information about detailed parental relationships and the presence of other adults in the household, such as unmarried partners, grandparents, and other relatives, is important for understanding children's social, economic, and developmental well-being. America's Children (2019) reports that while the majority of children live with two parents, many children have other living arrangements. For example, in 2018, 22% of children lived with their mothers only, 4% lived with their fathers only, and 4% lived with neither of their parents. Those children who lived with neither of their parents were reported as living with grandparents or other relatives.

Although there are biases in reporting and data collection, these demographics are likely to favor White, non-Hispanic, heterosexual families. Numbers of same-sex headed families, immigrant families, non-English or Spanish speaking families, and other marginalized populations are often underrepresented in largescale data collection that are dependent upon self-reporting. Additionally, due to census categories, more nuanced racial and ethnic identities, multi-racial, mixed race, gender non-conforming, multiple household families (step-parents and children), or polyamorous identities do not get included.

Instead of viewing children who have family structures other than the two-parent-family-living-under-one roof as the exception or aberrant, we need to shift our talk about family to include all of those people who are important caregivers to the child. Tschida and Buchanan (2017) argue that, "Disrupting the single story of family is important for both students who see themselves in different stories, and for students who may have never considered different compositions of family" (pp. 3–4). Therefore children's literature can perpetuate those singular notions of family or offer portrayals of families that more accurately mirrors their realities. The next section includes a checklist to use when selecting books for read alouds or classroom libraries, and is followed by recommendations of books with diverse families.

Checklist for Selecting Children's Literature

All books foreground certain characters and messages. These are the elements that initially draw readers to the text. Texts also include more subtle messages that serve to reinforce dominant ideologies or disrupt them. When selecting texts, there are no "good" or "bad" texts, rather, critical literacy explores how teachers engage students in critical conversations about representation, stereotypes, misconceptions, or tokenism, and encourages thoughtful, meaningful engagement with texts as cultural artifacts. Table 1 provides a checklist for considering children's literature selection.

Table 1. Checklist for Selecting Children's Literature with Diverse Families

Criteria	What to look for	Questions to Ask Yourself
Author and/or Illustrator	Background and perspective Diverse authors "Own voice" authors	Are you intentionally selecting books written and illustrated by diverse authors? Will this book allow children to learn about perspective taking and challenge their own assumptions of families? Is the author writing in their "own voice" as a member of a historically marginalized community of which a character is depicted?
Activity	Stereotypical gender roles Dominant/subordinate relationships	Do the characters engage in stereotypical gender roles or challenge heteronormative gender roles? What is the relationship between characters? Is one character in a position of power over another character? How does this positioning reinforce or disrupt stereotypes?
Appeal	Topic Characters Images/Illustrations Font	Many children's books have animals as the primary characters, however this does not make them immune to stereotypes or power dynamics. Do the characters depicted represent real people or are they anthropomorphized personas? What is the style or feel of the text? Is it in the style of a cartoon, or a collage of mixed media? Are there bright, bold colors or soft, fine lines? Is the font easy to read for emergent and novice readers?

Criteria	What to look for	Questions to Ask Yourself
Date	Date written Date published	Books are products of the time in which they were written and published. Representations of character, what they say, and do are contextual. Does this text reflect a dated cultural mindset or norm? If so, how have societal expectations or acceptance changed?
Family Constellation	Messages about different ways of living and relationships	What is the family constellation: single parent, same-sex headed family, multiple households, children who are adopted, mixed race families – parents and/or children, or intergenerational? How does the reader know which characters are in a romantic relationship? How does the reader know which characters are family?
Illustration and Identity	Race Religion Ethnicity Abilities Gender	How does the author and illustrator depict ethnicity, religion, abilities, or race? Is it by skin tone, clothing, housing, assistive devices, representations of wealth/poverty, food, names, or relationships between characters? Do these representations support stereotypes or challenge them? Are there identities that reflect tokenism or are conspicuously absent?
Language	Vocabulary Dialects Names Terms Language	Pronunciation of names is important. During a read aloud, how will you find the correct pronunciation of an unfamiliar name or term to students? When reading aloud, children love to hear characters speaking different voices. Are you speaking with an accent or dialect that is derogatory or stereotypical?

Criteria	What to look for	Questions to Ask Yourself
Living Arrangements	Location Housing	Where does the story take place? Is the community rural, urban, suburban? What are the primary housing structures (single family house, apartment building, farm)?

Recommendations for Books with Diverse Families

A Family Is a Family Is a Family by Sara O'Leary (2016). When a teacher asks her class to think about what makes their families special, students share about who they live with and who loves them, highlighting that families may look different but share the common characteristic of having caring people.

Double Trouble for Anna Hibiscus by Atinuke and Lauren Tobia (2015). Anna Hibiscus lives in Africa with her White mother, African father, cousins, uncles, aunties, and grandparents. She meets her twin brothers for the first time and adjusts to life with her new siblings.

I Love Saturday y domingos by Alma Flor Ada and Illustrated by Claudia Degliuomini (1999). We follow the narrator as she visits her Grandma and Grandpa who come from a European-American background on Saturdays and again on Sundays when she visits Abuelito y Abuelita, who are Mexican-American.

Last Stop on Market Street by Matt De La Pena and Illustrated by Christian Robinson (2015). CJ and his grandmother meet people in their community and learn to appreciate simplicity as they walk through the city and take a bus ride on their way to working at a soup kitchen.

One Family by George Shannon and Illustrated by Blanca Gomez (2015). A playful counting book that depicts diverse characters and cultural images.

Real Sisters Pretend by Megan Lambert (2016). Adopted sisters pretend-play and take care of one another's feelings as they talk about what it means to be sisters and part of a family.

Stella Brings the Family by Miriam Schiffer (2015). Stella, who has two dads, figures out how to celebrate her family during the class Mother's Day celebration.

Thunder Boy Jr. by Sherman Alexie and Illustrated by Yuyi Morales (2016). Thunder Boy is named after his father, but he wants his own name that he thinks would be more fitting.

We Are Family by Patricia Hegarty and Illustrated by Ryan Wheatcroft (2017). A rhyming book that depicts illustrations of various families engaging in life's activities.

Conclusion

As educators, we need to be intentional about the text choices we make. All curricular decisions are grounded in ideologies that serve various purposes. Children's literature serves as windows and mirrors to identity development and how children see themselves in a complex world. Since identities are intersectional, students need to be exposed to a range of family constellations, composed of diverse people, that allow for multiple representations. Through critical conversations about texts, students become more empowered to act upon the social and political issues that surround them, as well as challenging their biases (Vasquez, 2014). It is through these actions that teachers can act and dismantle problematic family norms in their classroom so that students can be respected, valued, and heard.

Discussion Questions

1. Why must we include books that represent diverse family constellations in our classrooms and school libraries?
2. After reading this chapter and reviewing the rubric on text selection, what will you now consider when reviewing children's books to determine their appropriateness for your classroom?

References

Apple, M. (2001). *Educating the "Right" way: Markets, standards, God, and inequity.* Routledge Falmer.

America's Children: Key National Indicators of Well-Being. (2019). https://www.childst ats.gov/

Barton, D., & Hamilton M. (1998). *Local literacies: Reading and writing in one community.* Routledge.

Bell, M. (2009). Valuing all families. *Law, Culture and the Humanities, 5*(2), 288–316. ISSN: 1743-8721.

Bishop, E. (2014). Critical literacy: Bringing theory to praxis. *Journal of Curriculum Theorizing, 30*(1), 51–63. https://journal.jctonline.org/index.php/jct/article/view/457

Bishop, R. S. (1990). Mirror, windows, and sliding glass doors. *Perspectives: Choosing and using books for the classrooms*, 6(3). Reprinted from original source. https://scenicr egional.org/wp-content/uploads/2017/08/Mirrors-Windows-and-Sliding-Glass-Doors.pdf

Casper, V., & Schultz, S. (1999). *Gay parents/straight schools: Building communication and trust*. Teachers College Press.

Chatters, L., Taylor, R., & Jayakody, R. (1994). Fictive kinship relations in black extended families. *Journal of Comparative Family Studies*, 25(3), 297–312. http://www.jstor.org/stable/41602341

Compton-Lilly, C. (2003). *Reading families: The literate lives of urban children*. Teachers College Press.

Compton-Lilly, C. (2004). *Confronting racism, poverty, and power: Classroom struggles to change the world*. Heinemann.

Derman-Sparks, L. (2016). *Guide for selecting anti-bias children's books*. https://socialj usticebooks.org/guide-for-selecting-anti-bias-childrens-books/

Gee, J. (2015). *Social linguistics and literacy: Ideology in discourses* (5th ed.). Routledge.

Ladson-Billings, G. (1994). *The Dreamkeepers: Successful teachers of African American children*. Jossey-Bass.

Landale, N., Oropesa R., & Bradatan C. (2006). Hispanic families in the United States: Family structure and process in an era of family change. In: M. Tienda & F. Mitchell (Eds.), *National research Council (US) panel on Hispanics in the United States: Hispanics and the future of America*. National Academies Press. https://www.ncbi.nlm.nih.gov/books/NBK19902/

Larrabee, T., & Kim, Y. (2010). Preservice elementary teachers' perceptions of family: Considering future instruction on lesbian- and gay-headed families. *Journal of Research in Children Education International*, *24*, 351–365. doi: https://doi.org/10.1080/02568543.2010.510085

Larson, J., & Marsh, J. (2015). *Making literacy real: Theories and practices for learning and teaching* (2nd ed.). Sage Publications.

Miller, H., Olmstead, K., Colantonio-Yurko, K., Shema, A., & Svrcek, N. (2020). Moving from inaction to action: Challenging homo- and transphobia in Middle School English Language Arts. *Middle Grades Review*, 6(1), Article 5. Available at: https://scholarworks.uvm.edu/mgreview/vol6/iss1/5

Rogoff, B. (2003). *The cultural nature of human development*. Oxford University Press.

Ryan, C., & Hermann-Wilmarth, J. (2018). *Reading the rainbow: LGBTQ-inclusive literacy instruction in the elementary classroom*. Teachers College Press.

Shannon, P. (1992). *Becoming political: Reading and writing in the politics of literacy education*. Heinemann.

Shema, A. (2015). *Troubling "Family": How primary grade teachers conceptualize family and normative construction of family in elementary schools* (Doctoral dissertation). Available from ProQuest Dissertations & Theses Global database. (UMI No. 3703283).

Street, B. (1995). *Social literacies: Critical approaches to literacy development, ethnography, and education.* Longham.

Surtees, N., & Gunn, A. (2010). (Re)marking heteronormativity: Resisting practices in early childhood education contexts. *Australian Journal of Early Childhood, 35*(1), 42–47.

Tschida, C., & Buchanan, L. (2017). What makes a family? Multiple perspectives in an inclusive text set. *Social Studies and the Young Learner, 30*(2), 3–7.

Tschida, C., Ryan, C., Ticknore, R., & Ticknore, A. (2014). Building on windows and mirrors: Encouraging the disruption of "single stories" through children's literature. *Journal of Children's Literature, 40*(1), 28–39.

Vasquez, V. (2014). *Negotiating critical literacies with young children.* Routledge.

Vasquez, V., Janks, H., & Comber, B. (2019). Critical literacy as a way of being and doing. *Language Arts, 96*(5), 300–310.

Weiss, H., Caspe, M., & Lopez, M. E. (2006). *Family involvement in early childhood education, Spring(1).* Harvard Family Research Project.

**Part Three Taking Action: Engaging
Students in Literature-Based
Discussions for Change**

6. Reflections on Disrupting Historic Understandings and White Lenses on Teacher Pedagogy & Practice

Dori Harrison & Holly Spinelli

Diverse student populations bring multiple perspectives into classroom settings (Sleeter, 2001). However, Sleeter reported that teacher education programs are often slow in their response to updating curriculum, addressing cultural gaps in teacher practice, and critically addressing whiteness in education. The same issues noted by Sleeter in 2001 are still present today. A challenge for colleges of education includes how to prepare a predominantly White field of educators for an ethnically and culturally diverse student population. Many studies report on ways programs and teachers have failed to address the gaps, but fewer studies have focused on the successful ways colleges and/or individual teachers have made small triumphs towards this end. In this chapter we highlight the reflective experiences of two educators, Holly a a 7-12 educator within the Northeast region of the United States and Dori, a professor who works in the Southeast region at a predominantly white institution that is also Christian based.

The preparation of teachers for diversity within the classroom and community has many implications for practice. Teacher preparation cannot be separated from the ways in which beginning teachers enter the field. Ladson-Billings (2001) helped paint the picture of the layers of diversity that teachers encounter in schools— many for the first time. Ladson-Billings described linguistic diversity, racial and ethnic diversity, and varying conditions associated with coming from a lower socioeconomic status. Milner (2010) echoes this sentiment. While teacher education programs are providing the theoretical foundations to call for multicultural perspectives this does not always result in a change in practice. Milner (2010) calls for "teaching practices that will ultimately need to be expanded and interrogated" (p. 125). That is the charge we present here.

The frameworks from which we pull our understanding of antiracist pedagogy includes a combination of several definitions and perspectives (i.e. Banks & Banks, 2016). Like Kailin (1998) we argue that, "Antiracists adhere to the view that racism is an integral feature of the educational system and that it manifests itself habitually" (p. 81).

Purpose

The purpose of this chapter is to provide a better understanding of the ways teacher education programs can move beyond theoretical explanations of diversity into action, as well as the ways teachers can move beyond the role of ally and advocate for their students and colleagues. In order to fulfill this purpose, we focus on two reflective cases from our own teaching experiences. The first case discusses efforts preparing pre-service teachers. The second case discusses strategies used to cultivate antiracist and anti-bias frameworks within ourselves and our classroom environments. Both perspectives are informed by our identities as teachers who are linguistically and culturally diverse. Our pedagogical approaches to teaching have strong antiracist and equity agendas. However, our reflections will highlight the juxtaposition of our antiracist approaches alongside the predominately White teaching environments. A key aspect of our work is our own consciousness and knowledge in dealing with issues of race within the teaching profession.

We begin by focusing on the foundations of our pedagogical approaches—antiracist pedagogy. It is imperative that readers of this work understand what fuels our call toward antiracist work before presenting our reflections.

Antiracist Pedagogy

Antiracist pedagogy has its early foundation in the 1980s with the rise of critical pedagogy. Over time, researchers determined that the purpose of antiracist pedagogy should be aimed at transformation by challenging the individual and the structural system that perpetuates racism (Taylor, 2017; Utt & Tochluk, 2020; Wagner, 2005; Giroux, 2004). Antiracist pedagogy seeks to dismantle oppressive systems and the powers that perpetuate racist systems. It provides a framework to reimagine how institutions prepare our future teachers. Antiracist pedagogy equips practicing teachers with pedagogical approaches to make their classrooms accessible and transformative spaces of learning.

Next, we highlight key studies that have influenced our antiracist pedagogical approaches.

Examining Racialized Discomfort

Nieto (1996) found that, historically, the field of education saw no need to engage students in difficult conversations and was comfortable with maintaining multicultural approaches. If discomfort should be a part of learning, then we must introduce the concept of discomfort to preservice teachers. A study by Ohito (2016) attests to the continued pattern of whiteness within the field of education. The study examined the emotional reactions of preservice teachers when they were made uncomfortable during antiracist teaching; what Ohito called racialized discomfort. Within the study Ohito and students monitored their emotional states when discussing issues of race within the course. They discussed and addressed issues of discomfort within the class and through reflective activities. Ultimately, White preservice teachers became comfortable with their discussions of race and racism within the context of their learning.

Antiracist Professional Development

Antiracist educators must be prepared to "challenge the institutional as well as structural system that perpetuates racism" (Ohito, 2020, p. 30). Because many programs have yet to adopt an antiracist position, finding opportunities to create additional training for practicing teachers should also be considered. Specifically, professional development opportunities for teachers should also be aligned with an antiracist pedagogical stance. McManimon and Casey (2018) noticed a lack of emphasis on structural racism within professional development programs for teachers. What they did notice were calls for equitable education initiatives which did not address the role of race or racism in schools. Utilizing bell hooks (1994) conceptualization of theory as a liberatory practice, the researchers grounded each session in education theory and moved participants towards deeper understanding on the institutionalized nature of racism and whiteness in education. By having participants continually study, reflect, and take action, the participants were able to share their growth and understanding of their whiteness as well as take steps to make their classrooms more equitable.

Use of Diverse Literature

Neville (2020) found that the inclusion of diverse texts in teacher education programs are often insufficient. Over the course of Neville's study, students engaged in guided critical discussions of images and books that included broader themes around racial and societal issues. Diverse literature is a tool, but it needs to have well equipped guides to help students with the diverse themes and contexts that may arise during their interaction with the text. In Neville's work, teachers learned to trace their learning and positionalities across texts that addressed issues of race, power, and oppression (p. 205).

The Power of Narrative

In education, narratives are valued as a part of reflection. They offer representational practices that mediate the structures of social power at various levels (in academia and K-12) and across regions (southeast and northeast) which are hypothesized to be progressively different. We recognize the power of stories to challenge racist characterizations of cultures and groups (Solorzano & Yosso, 2002). In our narratives, we focus on the ways we've understood and enacted antiracist work in academia and K-12 settings. We offer two reflective stories of anti-racist pedagogical approaches from within a teacher education program and as educators in the field. The next two sections present our reflections of teaching using antiracist pedagogical approaches.

Dori's Reflection: Disrupting Approaches to "Seeing" Our Students Through Dirty Lenses

I am an African American woman who was raised in the South. My reflections are based on teaching at a small liberal arts institution in Tennessee. I worked with undergraduate and graduate students during their student teaching experiences. As an African American female instructor, I tasked myself with the responsibility of providing student teachers with diverse experiences at their placements in the city approximately two to fifteen miles from the college. I wanted to teach the course in a way that highlighted the gaps in student teachers' cultural understanding and provided opportunities for them to notice the institutionalized racism present at their placements.

My educational experiences and personal history are embedded within this city. I grew up in the city and am a product of the curriculum taught within the schools. It wasn't until I went away to college that I realized how much I didn't know about my own culture or the cultures across my state. I then returned to my city and taught for eight years. I believe that the best teachers come into the classroom with lived understandings of cultural competency versus reading it in a book or watching a film. My reflective narrative captures the ways I began noticing race and the ways I now embed antiracist practices of navigating racialized discomfort (Ohito, 2016) to enable teacher candidates to understand various cultures through activities (e.g. inviting students to visit important community sites and engage with members of the community).

Dirty Lenses

In 2009, I recall sitting in my own teacher education program and hearing about urban students' learning and performance histories. Preservice teachers, who were predominately White, described the hypothesized learning gaps present between Black and White students, however, there were no moments of clarity offered. Professors failed to counter the deficit narratives that were perpetuated in conversations. Some of my classmates' lenses toward the educational landscape were jaded and dirty. Meritocracy and an unwillingness to work hard were often at the heart of comments about Black and Brown people without taking into consideration the oppressive and systemic barriers that produced such difference. Over time, as I and others began to share our experiences in education and the lives our families lived, there was a realization that meritocracy is not a theory that can justify why those in poverty have difficulty coming out of their economic surroundings. However, this took multiple examples coming from those within the community as it was not learned through engagement with literature alone. This approach, unfortunately, places unneeded responsibility on the people of color within the course which can also be damaging.

Spaces of education should offer ways to clean those lenses by encouraging critical thinking and providing approaches to understanding the world. Encouraging student teachers to problematize preconceived notions about their students can also be helpful. These lenses are not made clear with one session in a course or one class. In the same way it takes multiple wipes with a solution or cloth to clean our glasses, it takes multiple wipes with a solution to develop clear perspectives informed by research and experience.

Teacher Education Programs

In my experience in higher education, teacher education programs try to fit culturally relevant pedagogy into one lesson within a 16-week semester. In order for future educators to see our Black and Brown students beyond data and media representations, teacher education programs and their faculty must increase efforts to immerse preservice teachers in meaningful antiracist experiences throughout their learning. In general, the field of teaching continues to highlight classroom diversity and culturally responsive practice within their curriculum. Thus, a goal of preservice teacher education programs must be to (1) increase student awareness of the community, (2) learn ways to disrupt colonized practices, pedagogies, and materials, and (3) to have an unwavering commitment to diverse communities. These three goals are based on the idea that teacher education programs will move beyond the guise of advocacy into a space of true commitment to the multiple communities in which teachers serve. This leads to two questions:

1. How is this goal realized within preservice teaching?
2. What are some approaches to thinking about student teachers' early experiences in the field?

Here, I report on reflective data from one academic semester of a course I taught for student teachers. Twenty-three student teachers were enrolled in the course across license areas, fourteen were graduate students and nine were undergraduate students. Of these students, three identified as Latinx and the remaining students identified as White. The course was predominantly female, with only one male student. The demographics of the class was similar to the national trend of an average 80% White female workforce (Loewus, 2017; Ladson-Billings, 2001). These factors guided both my thinking and my approach to helping students realize that their understanding of diversity in education needed to be challenged and transformed.

Ideologies about race and place. One goal for the course was to help students understand how their university learning would translate into classroom practice. Part of that understanding involved their interactions with diverse groups of students and their families. At the beginning of the course, students are introduced to the concept of bias in the context of teacher practice. What came about from the conversation was an understanding of urban schools through a deficit lens. Student teachers recalled learning that children of color in the urban schools lacked parental support, that teaching was harder in linguistically diverse spaces, and they made generalizations about African American students as loud and lacking structure. Student teachers in my course assumed students were poor due to drug use by parents, and that violent language was a part of Black culture.

As a Black female educator, I was appalled by their statements. I taught in the local schools and knew families of children still attending the schools being described. I was forced to reflect on their statements. I had to ignore the social justice warrior that wanted to scream, "ARE YOU SERIOUS?" from the rooftop. I quickly realized student teachers knew multicultural and transformative theories and pedagogies, however, they were unable to apply them to their descriptions of the culturally and linguistically diverse children in the K-12 schools. The obvious cultural discontinuity (Blakeney, 2005) which existed in their responses lingered with me. Unlike previous studies of cultural discontinuity, this case embodied a disconnect between me – an African American faculty member – with the predominately White student teachers. This knowledge and awareness drove me to re-design elements of the course through antiracist pedagogical practices. Below, I detail some of the strategies I used within the course.

Thinking deeply and critically. Part of a student teacher's charge in my course is to realize that how they have grown up has shaped their view of the world. The second part of that realization is to seek out the truth in the stories they have been told over time. To accomplish this goal, I developed questions that required them to think about the narratives formed in their classrooms, the narratives in media, and the theoretical narratives they have been taught by instructors in their teacher education program. Student teachers had to use the language of theory to explain what they had observed during class discussions. First, we began with Frank's (1999) ethnographic eyes. This approach would help students conceptualize learning, knowledge, and diversity in their classrooms by having pre-service teachers learn to recognize patterns in their thinking. In addition, preservice teachers begin moving their observations into impressions of students and learning. This approach was also coupled with bell hooks' (1994) concept of theory development in education. For example, aspects of hook's (1994) work focuses on holistic education, the well-being of students, and critically reflecting on culture, gender, race, and class with regard to our teaching. We applied these approaches to student teachers' classroom observations, but also to their observations in the community at large.

In the beginning of the course, discussions fell flat. Students were resistant, or possibly hesitant, to take up antiracist ways of thinking about teacher practice. One sentiment expressed by students was a feeling that the concepts being discussed were repetitive of past courses when they first learned about culturally responsive and culturally relevant pedagogy. I worked to overcome this resistance with students by using an approach described by Neville (2020). I had students first interrogate their positions and the histories they "knew" to be true. We created small book groups using texts that addressed inequities in education; from theory to practice. In addition, students were assigned critical thinking prompts associated with their books and their field experiences. The field experience journals were designed to have student teachers think and find moments that might challenge their previous learning as when thinking critically about our personal history within the larger context of education and the community, we often find misconceptions related to our future classrooms. Below I list some of the questions used with student teachers:

- Which communication styles are valued in the classroom setting, and how does this match with your students' backgrounds and experiences?
- Which categories of diversity are most comfortable for you to teach? Which categories are least comfortable?
- Are you a cultural outsider or insider at your school? (Hint: we are all outsiders) What steps have you taken to learn more about the community?
- Which ethnic and racial cultures are present in your classroom? Do students' behaviors match with the media depictions of their culture? How does this inform or impair your instruction?
- How many authors of color do you introduce within your instruction across disciplines?

After going through the process of reflecting on the questions and engaging in discussions, the student teachers became more thoughtful about their choices in the classroom. For example, a student reflected on the cultural disconnect between the diverse students in her classroom. She described ways she began to see herself as a cultural outsider who was still learning the community. This was a drastic difference from earlier descriptions of student behavior as loud and impulsive in the classroom. In another student example, she made connections to Bronfenbrenner's Ecological Systems Theory, no longer seeing student behavior and action as separate from their culture, history, and environment. Student teachers who failed to "dig deep" into their own thinking stood out within these conversations and/or written responses as they questioned whether racism still existed and rarely contributed in the class without explicitly being asked to do so.

Discovering new narratives. A prominent theme for the course was how to think critically about our instruction as it related to the P-12 students. It was my belief that this type of critical thinking could not take place unless the preservice teachers being taught were aware of their own biases and judgements of students. To help accomplish this goal, I needed the candidates to realize how their perspectives were informed by their past experiences. To continue removing layers of dirt from their lenses, I provided them with community-based experiences with different organizations. For example, we visited an organization focused on helping young teenagers who were homeless or struggling. Student teachers toured and learned about community partnerships between schools and non-profit youth services. They engaged with volunteers and discovered what children in these situations could do and accomplish with the right support. Due to the religious unrest within the community, we took time to visit an Islamic center to get to know the community. While there, students learned of racist and discriminatory actions that some parents experienced within the school system. As teachers, we learn from community narratives in order to better serve the students in our classrooms.

The choices of field trips for the class was based upon conversations with the student teachers about their experiences and information gleaned from their reflections. Some guiding questions included:

- Which communities of people are we least familiar with in our classrooms?
- Which religious cultures are we least familiar with in our classrooms?
- How can we learn more about our students' lives in the community?

The trips we took during the semester served as a bridge between theory and practice. They were transformative— serving as counter narratives, and helping student teachers develop new narratives. I did not abandon the multicultural tenets of the course. However, I did shift away from notions of tolerance to focus on enabling student teachers to provide evidence that contradicted some previously held notions. For example, instead of allowing the student teachers to simply state they notice other cultures and languages that are different, we took time to place ourselves in multicultural community spaces in order to learn. The trips challenged some students to enter worlds in which they were unfamiliar. By placing students within these lived experiences, they were able to engage with cultures of people who they may have actively or subconsciously avoided otherwise. By sharing this account, my hope is for colleges of education to move beyond discussions of cultural competence into immersions of community experiences. Our future teachers will continue to live in a state of fear and distrust for the unknown unless we strategically include moments of discomfort across the curriculum.

Taking Action

Many teachers live away from the communities in which they work. Take time to know the community and your students. While you can look up demographic information online, you won't understand the heart of the community until you place your feet on the ground. You can begin with the following:

- Learn about after school programs. These are great resources for getting you connected with how students spend their time outside of school. This applies primarily to elementary schools.
- Connect with the district representative.
- Take a drive or two through the community on the weekends.
- Attend a local church or temple to learn more about the culture.
- Use social media to learn about the local events.
- Ask seasoned and tenured teachers about the dynamics of the community and ways the school engages with the community.
- Make time for home visits with your students; virtual or in person.
- Connect with the parent teacher organization prior to coming onboard.

Taking these steps helps us show dedication to the community and embodies an understanding that the teaching profession should be embedded within the communities we serve. Through the process of becoming aware of the systemic racism that is part of education in the United States and other nations, we can move into ways of wiping our lenses clean. We must become invested in removing years and years of dirt that has prevented us from seeing our students and seeking to understand their worlds before we step foot into our classrooms. It takes perseverance and continued learning to have success with these methods.

Holly's Reflection: Teaching in and Beyond Inclusive Professional Communities

I am an Italian-American woman who currently teaches reading and writing at a public high school and a public community college in the Hudson Valley of New York. My personal educational experiences and my professional focus are deeply rooted in public education. New York is my home state, and my own K-12 educational experience took place in its public schools. My reflections are based on teaching and learning in New York's urban and suburban public high schools.

I recognized at a young age that the literary canon excluded or misrepresented many facets of my own upbringing, such as being raised by a single-parent, living in a dwelling with family that spans generations and literacy acquisition, growing up with friends from various cultural and linguistic backgrounds, and being a first-generation four-year university student. My reflective narrative encompasses my realization that an inclusive, culturally responsive education is one rooted in educators' communities, actions, and choices. This became apparent when I transitioned from teaching in a progressive, experiential public school in New York City, to teaching at a public school in Westchester County, one of New York City's most affluent suburbs. The cultural shift was profound. It forced me to confront the importance of my pedagogical approaches to conversations, lessons, and course materials about race, intersectionality, and inclusivity, even if it meant breaking tradition, challenging the literary canon, and teaching with discomfort. I believed that my students deserved to see themselves, as well as those they may have never met, represented in the texts and materials we studied together. I wanted to provide opportunities and actionable practices for students and colleagues to recognize and challenge their own respective teaching and learning in ways that are culturally and linguistically affirming and inclusive, even at the expense of their own or others' comfort.

From 2015 to 2020, approximately one-third of the way through my teaching career, I made a life transition that took me outside of New York City's boroughs, away from my trusted colleagues in the high school setting, and dropped me in a new high school with a predominantly White student and educator population. When I first arrived in the affluent suburban school, over 95% of the student population was classified as "White" and the staff was almost equally represented by White educators. I knew this would be different from my previous professional and educational experiences, but I didn't fully understand how the differences would unfold until it began.

Reflecting on the Curriculum

At first, I was slated to teach two sections of 9th grade Regents-level English, two sections of 10th grade Honors English, and one 11th grade Regents-level English course. When I was introduced to the grade-level curricula, I was paralyzed by its stark, traditional nature. Almost every text was canonical; even the contemporary selections were written by and featured White males. Students and scholars would argue that this is more common than what I experienced early in my career. "Reconstructing the Canon," from the *Harvard Political Review* (2018), examines traditional high school students' experiences with canonical texts in classrooms across America:

> Regardless of a school's socioeconomic, cultural, or racial demographics, its curriculum is likely to be made up of books like *The Adventures of Huckleberry Finn*, *The Scarlet Letter*, and *Catcher in the Rye*. These books share several traits: they were all written by white, heterosexual, dead males. While these

books have literary merit and provide high school students with shared cultural references, the homogeneity of their authors and characters provides a canon that fails to cater to a heterogeneous audience. (Black, 2018)

In my first year of teaching in a suburban environment, there were few female authors and very few Black, Indigenous, or people of color (BIPOC) authors listed on the prescribed 9th, 10th, and 11th grade-level curriculum maps, which served as the guides for the courses I was assigned to teach. The female and BIPOC authors and texts mostly appeared in the senior-level and elective courses. My heart sank and I had a *What have I gotten myself into?* crisis. I would be lying if I said this uneasiness was short-lived, but once the shock wore off, I made an active decision to work through it. I did not do this perfectly. I made many mistakes along the way. It wasn't easy, but I had to start somewhere. I've made significant progress, and I had to keep moving forward. The following suggestions are based off of my experiences and offer a way to reflect on the curriculum in your own school:

- Speak with grade-level colleagues about texts **beyond the canon** that they've taught or are interested in teaching.
- Ask **students** about the kinds of stories, texts, and social issues that pique their interests.
- **Reach out** to colleagues beyond your school district for strategies, resources, and ideas

Taking Action Through Common Ground with Colleagues and Students

The road to change was intimidating, but the more I followed my plan, the more I recognized that there were other educators in the building who shared similar interests. I started by meeting with the 12th grade team to discuss their text selections. Many of them shared contemporary texts, namely poets, who were people of color and, importantly, living writers. Their curricula featured living authors. I, too, wanted to introduce students to living authors' works. The senior educators and I exchanged ideas about texts by poets like Martín Espada, Tracy K. Smith, Ada Limón, and Joy Harjo. After recognizing that these authors were already present in other educators' curricula in the building, I took action.

I was not in a position where I could completely toss aside the prescribed curriculum, especially in the first few years in a new district—I was untenured and much of the school's culture was still unfamiliar to me. So, I initiated change with what I like to call the "small bites" approach. I started with centering the students' voices, interests, lived experiences, and ideas. I asked students what they wanted to learn. They were interested in exploring contemporary texts. My students recognized that I took their interests and experiences seriously. As a result, we were able to establish a community of mutual respect and trust. This helped me make pedagogical and curricular choices in a gradual de-centering of the canon. I built-in daily "Quick Write" sessions (three-five minutes a day) where students responded in writing to such prompts as:

- A social or global issue I'd like to learn more about is_____ _____ because_____.
- A subject or an author I've heard about but know little about is_____ _____.
- I'd like to learn_____ about the subject/writer because_____.
- When I hear terms like "gentrification" or "Black Lives Matter" I wonder_____ because_____.
- When I hear terms like "racism", "homophobia", "transphobia", or "sexism", I think_____.
- When I read _____, I see that _____ benefits within/beyond the text because_____.
- I learn most of my information about race and identity from_____ _____ and I'd like to try to learn from other sources. I'd like to learn more about sources like_____.

Initially, the conversations rendered little movement beyond the surface-level, but establishing a classroom environment where students feel safe in their vulnerability and safe in their learning and uncertainty quickly moved the conversations to much deeper levels. The language I used played a major role in co-creating this environment. I'd explain, "This is a school, a place to learn, not the place where we already know everything." "We can't learn unless we ask." I'd remind students, and myself, "If we're unsure, we state it and ask for help or ways to learn more." When students saw that I was okay with unpacking difficult questions, and that my room was a place where asking to learn rather than inspecting a text for a correct response is the norm, their trust in me, and for one another, quickly grew.

Disrupting Curriculum

While continuing to establish communal trust, I introduced students to short texts: poems, short stories, non-fiction articles, photographs, and two-four minute online videos, to help us unpack the issues from our daily Quick Write prompts. Over time, those smaller texts turned into the centered stories in my classroom. Yes, the texts were small, but the powerful discussions and the learning therein was tremendous. The canonical texts I was "required" to cover became supplemental to works written by women, non-gender conforming folks, and BIPOCs. Dominant narratives and whiteness were not the central focus in my classroom; however, I did not and I still do not ignore required texts. Instead, I restructure their place in students' learning, and I reframe the lenses through which my students and I discuss them. I apply approaches and lenses I taught in my previous educational space — that of Maxine Greene's (2000) philosophy of placing value on the arts and imagination — to help students (re)imagine their role in their learning, in the world as it is, and how they imagine it to be (Greene 2000). Greene's lens couples well with pedagogical approaches from the #DisruptTexts resources – whose BIPOC co-creators crafted to reframe the canon through social and cultural critiques. The #DisruptTexts resources helped me develop entry points and critical questions to help my students and colleagues talk about the canon's (ir)relevance to students' lives, the texts and intended (but not always accurate) universal themes. It also helped us consider why some texts and characters are problematic, the biases and oppressive systems that exist within the authors' intentions and time periods, and how we, as modern readers, compare the concepts and ideas presented in these texts to larger, national and global contemporary issues. Once my students saw that the curriculum was something they could challenge, critique, and compare to their own lives and their own world, the small bites of literature that helped frame the course work became equally as satisfying to engage with the larger canonical texts that they were expected to digest. A resource I've recently included in pairing or replacing canonical texts in my classroom is #TheBookChat. #TheBookChat's co-founders host Twitter chats where readers and educators discuss and share insights on texts and authors beyond the canon. This resource provides valuable interactive spaces where educators can collaborate across local, state, national, and global communities.

Discussion

We end this chapter with some practical insights to inform antiracist pedagogical approaches to teaching. Individually, we noticed the common themes among how we positioned ourselves, as well as how we were positioned within our respective institutions. Our individual positions intersect – an African American woman who occupied the position of a professor with more than ten years teaching experience, and a White woman who began her teaching career in a school with a long-established, culturally inclusive community – because we are both pedagogues of antiracist work who were new to traditional, white-centered spaces that focus on multicultural approaches to learning.

What we were able to glean from our shared/respective narratives concern the intersections of race, power, and agency. We both had power— the force/willingness to perform an act, in the choices we made to insert antiracist work within our teaching. The agency, the capacity or capability to do something, resides in our ability to make these changes within our first year in our individual classrooms. Yet, there were noticeable differences in how we experienced power and agency given our racial identities. As Dorian noted, much of her work was done in relative isolation, while Holly found support from the larger school community when implementing antiracist frameworks. Holly acted as an individual and was able to lead her changes using her own voice, knowledge, and lived experiences. Dorian, being from the local community, still found it necessary to pair with community voices to enact similar changes to do this apart from her colleagues. And so, we are left to conclude that although educators may occupy positions and are positioned in ways that embody power and agency to create changes, these changes can and will be experienced differently based upon race.

In our collective experience, we recognize that there are significant commonalities among teacher education programs and entering the teaching profession in K-12 classrooms. These educational spaces are deeply rooted in White dominant narratives, experiences, and perspectives. After navigating these spaces as students and professionals, we recognize the importance of educating ourselves, our colleagues, and our students about identifying, interrogating, and taking action to dismantle the profession's White-dominant status quo. Moreover, we acknowledge that applying these lenses and taking actionable steps to do so requires participants to experience varying degrees of difficulty, and thus, we must lean into the pedagogy of discomfort (Ohito, 2016) so that we can build culturally responsive, inclusive classroom spaces for all. As we work towards this endeavor, we must highlight that antiracist approaches within the classroom and the larger educational environment are not exhaustive. This work requires continuous self-reflection, openness to difficult or uncomfortable conversations, and frequent engagement with managing ideological diversity versus lived diversity within and beyond the classroom.

How Can We Get Our Students to Think More Critically About How They See the World?

As educators, we must model different learning strategies, including those in which we are not comfortable, so our students can see authentic learning in progress. It is critical that students are recognized as complex persons with unique lived experiences and their own areas of expertise. Students will learn to think more critically about how they see the world, if their thoughts, experiences, and ideas are treated with respect and dignity. This builds a safe environment where students move beyond an invitation to engage in critical thinking about their own views and ideas, and step into a role where they lead the conversations to do so. Students can do this successfully if they have educators who help them foster connections among their educational experiences, personal and cultural identities, and their future planning. As educators, it is important for us to help students understand that their individual perspective is one of millions in the world. As such, we must move beyond learning to find the "correct" answers. It is imperative that we assist students with building a desire to simultaneously learn how to create and engage in meaningful and inclusive practices, and unlearn harmful, oppressive thinking and behaviors. This can happen when educators invite students and one another to actively participate in moving beyond "tradition" when selecting authors, texts, and assignments, so that entire educational communities, namely those that are student-centered, learn and grow·with the world around them as they begin molding it to what they wish it to be.

Implications for practice

This is not a "how to" account, rather our suggestions will hopefully provide you with a few steps that will help orient you with thinking and acting as antiracist educators. It is critical to remember that antiracist teaching is on-going, not a destination. As such, it is critical for pre-service educators and current educators in the field to learn from and about the communities in which they will be teaching. They must become actively engaged with and committed to continuous antiracist and anti-bias work, which includes involvement with their school's broader communities, so that they can create genuinely inclusive educational spaces for all.

Suggested Readings and Online Resources

- Leonard, J. (2011). Using Bronfenbrenner's ecological theory to understand community partnerships: An historical case study of one urban high school. *Urban Education.* DOI: 0042085911400337.
- Ayers, W. (1995). *To become a teacher: Making a difference in children's lives.*
  This text helps educators identify and understand the importance of students exploring, studying, and including the arts and imagination across levels and disciplines in education.
- Jewell, T. (2020). *This book is anti-racist: 20 lessons on how to wake up, take action, and do the work.*
  This nonfiction text can engage K-12 educators and students alike. It includes vibrant illustrations with definitions, prompts, and lessons that help readers move towards actionable antiracist work. It helps readers explore racism and racial oppression's origins.
- Liu, M. (2013). Disrupting teacher education. Retrieved from: https://www.educationnext.org/disrupting-teacher-education
- Abolitionist Book Club:
  https://sites.google.com/view/abolitionistteachingbookclub/home
  Inspired by the work of Dr. Bettina Love and others, educators and scholars gather to discuss antiracist work that is still needed across colleges and K-12 schools alike. There are opportunities for professional development, resources, and ways of contacting experts in the field.
- Beyond the Canon http://www.beyondthecanon.com/team
  The Founder of Beyond The Canon, Simeilia Hodge-Dallaway, chronicles, catalogues, and produces plays that are written and performed by culturally diverse playwrights from around the world.
- #DisruptTexts
  The co-creators of this website and Twitter handle are female BIPOC educators who actively engage in critical thinking and meaningful dialogue around de-centering and re-thinking canonical texts in classrooms. Their work explores meaningful and engaging ways to help readers dig beyond the surface with inclusive reading, writing, and thinking practices within and beyond the classroom. They offer frameworks to help audiences "disrupt" or interrogate the literary canon.
- #ownvoices
  This Twitter hashtag distinguishes texts with characters and authors from underrepresented groups. More specifically, this delineation helps audiences identify texts where the marginalized community, culture, or group represented in the story is written from the perspective of

an author who identifies with or has the lived experiences of the same culture, community, or group.
- #TheBookChat
  The co-founders, Scott Bayer and Joel Garza, host monthly Twitter chats where participants discuss a variety of contemporary texts and authors. This digital resource is an excellent way for folks, namely educators, to broaden text types, reading experiences, and literary voices, while creating meaningful dialogue around literature and its relationship to race and social issues.

Discussion Questions

1. Reflect on your own teacher education experience. Is/was antiracist pedagogy a component of your program? If so, how did/does it influence your practice? If not, what do you think is the reason for its absence?
2. Evaluate the language you use and the environment you create in the classroom. Does it promote a safe and engaging space for all learners?

References

Alderman, D., Perez, R. N., Eaves, L. E., Klein, P., & Munoz, S. (2019). Reflections on operationalizing an anti-racism pedagogy: Teaching as regional storytelling. *Journal of Geography in Higher Education*. https://doi.org/10.1080/03098 265.2019.1661367

Banks, J., & Banks, C. A. (2016). *Multicultural Education: Issues and Perspectives*. Wiley.

Black, D. (2018). Reconstructing the canon. *The Harvard Political Review*. https://harv ardpolitics.com/culture/thecanon/.

Blakeney, A. M. (2005). Antiracist pedagogy: Definition, theory, and professional development. *Journal of Curriculum and Pedagogy*, 2(1), 119–132.

Frank, C. (1999). Ethnographic eyes: A teacher's guide to classroom observation. Portsmouth, NH: Heinemann.

Giroux, H. A. (2004). Public pedagogy and the politics of neo-liberalism: Making the political more pedagogical. *Policy Futures in Education*, 2(3–4), 494–503.

Greene, M. (2000). *Releasing the imagination: Essays on education, the arts, and social change* (pp. 188–189; 197–198).

Hinton, M., & Ono-George, M. (2019). Teaching a history of "race" and anti-racist action in an academic classroom. *Area 00*, 1–6. Retrieved from https://doi.org/ 10.1111/area.12536

hooks, b. (1994). *Teaching to transgress: Education as the practice of freedom*. New York: Routledge.

Kailin, J. (1998). Preparing urban teachers for schools and communities: an anti-racist perspective. *High School Journal, 82* (2), 80-88.

Kandaswamy, P. (2007). Beyond colorblindness and multiculturalism: Rethinking anti-racist pedagogy in the university classroom. *Radical Teacher, 80,* 6–11.

Kishimoto, K. (2018). Anti-racist pedagogy: From faculty's self-reflection to organizing within and beyond the classroom. *Race Ethnicity and Education, 21*(4), 540–554.

Ladson-Billings, G. (2001*). Crossing over to Canaan: The journey of new teachers in diverse classrooms.* San Francisco, CA: Jossey-Bass.

Loewus, L. (2017). *The nation's teaching force is still mostly white and female. https://www. edweek.org/ew/articles/2017/08/15/the-nations-teaching-force-is-still-mostly.html*

McManimon, S. K., & Casey, Z. A. (2018). (Re)beginning and becoming: Antiracism and professional development with white practicing teachers. *Teaching Education, 29*(4), 395–406.

Milner IV, H. R. (2010). What does teacher education have to do with teaching? Implications for diversity studies. *Journal of Teacher Education, 61*(1–2), 118–131.

National Center for Educational Statistics. (2017). https://nces.ed.gov/programs/rac eindicators/spotlight_a.asp.

Neville, M. L. (2020). 'I can't believe I didn't learn this in school': 'refusing secondly' as an anti-racist English education framework. *Changing English, 27*(2), 193–207.

Nieto, S. (1996). *Affirming diversity: The sociopolitical context of multicultural education (2nd ed.).* White Plains, NY: Longman Publisher.

Ohito, E. O. (2020). Fleshing out enactments of Whiteness in antiracist pedagogy: Snapshots of a White teacher educator's practice. *Pedagogy, Culture & Society, 28*(1), 17–36.

Ohito, E. O. (2016). Making the Emperor's New Clothes visible in anti-racist teacher education: Enacting a pedagogy of discomfort with white preservice teachers. *Equity & Excellence in Education, 49*(4), 454–467.

Phillips, J. A., Risdon, N., Lamsma, M., Hambrick, A., & Jun, A. (2019). Barriers and strategies by white faculty who incorporate anti-racist pedagogy. *Race & Pedagogy, 3*(2), 1–27.

Sleeter, C. (2001). Preparing teachers for culturally diverse schools: Research and the overwhelming presence of whiteness. *Journal of Teacher Education, 52*(2), 94–106.

Solórzano, D.G. and Yosso, T.J. (2002) Critical race methodology: Counter-story-telling as an analytical framework for education research. *Qualitative Inquiry, 8,* 23–44.

Taylor, A. M. (2017). Teaching while white: White identity development and antiracism for educators. *Master's Projects and Capstones, 513.* https://repository.usfca.edu/capstone/513.

Utt, J., & Tochluk, S. (2020). White teacher, know thyself: Improving anti-racist praxis through racial identity development. *Urban Education, 55*(1), 125–152.

Wagner, A. E. (2005). Unsettling the academy: Working through the challenges of anti-racist pedagogy. *Race Ethnicity and Education, 8*(3), 261–275.

7. Anti-racist Teaching Using Young Adult Literature

Shelby Boehm & Mario Worlds

Racial inequity and disparities within schools continue to reflect those seen throughout the larger society. Educators, particularly English Language Arts (ELA) teachers, must strongly consider how their teaching practices answer Freire's (1972, 1984) call to provide educational spaces that promote equity and justice. Additionally ELA teachers must provide students with critical literacy skills that help them challenge racial inequities. If educators are to seriously combat racial inequality, teaching practices must move away from deracialized modes of education in favor of anti-racist pedagogies that more accurately and directly address issues of race and racism that are structurally engrained within schools and across the globe (Troyna, 2006).

To that end, ELA classrooms have long represented spaces where educators have used literary tools such as young adult literature (YAL) to address issues of race, culture, society, sexuality, and class, among others. However, we argue that given the current racial climate seen not just within the United States but also across the globe, ELA educators must take full advantage of the wide range of YAL that can be used to challenge dominant discourses of race and cultivate ways of reading the world through an anti-racist lens. Anti-racist educators seek to confront and dismantle institutional racism that serves as the foundational structure for many schools (Tator & Henry, 1991, p. 145).

We argue that young adult literature, which speaks to the youthful experiences of students, can be used to create learning spaces where historical and contemporary reasons for ongoing racial inequality can be explored. Both authors are former English language arts teachers who utilized young adult literature to discuss critical issues alongside their students. Mario is a cisgender Black male. He has conducted research on the historical impact of anti-black racism in literacy education and the need for anti-racist teaching. Shelby is a cisgender white female. She used anti-racist book clubs featuring YAL with her tenth grade students, who read these texts alongside inquiry projects based on socio-political issues.

In this chapter, we offer a number of texts, such as *The Hate U Give* by Angie Thomas (2017) and *All American Boys* by Jason Reynolds and Brendan Kiely (2015) that can be used to help students recognize racial discrimination as a systematic problem that is actualized through policies and practices. Additionally, we offer strategies that can be used alongside the reading of the suggested texts to provide opportunities for students to engage in dialogical encounters that promote the changing of existing perceptions and racial ideologies in exchange for newly discovered knowledge and outlooks on the world (Mayo, 1999). We argue that using the previously listed texts combined with suggested activities and discussions help teachers and educators graduate from the limiting possibilities of multicultural education and literature and develop more critical approaches to teaching and learning. More specifically, we contend that through the texts' centering of race and race related discussions, teachers are better equiped to utlize anti-racist pedagogies that directly speak to the racialized experiences of students from under represented student populations.

Literature Review

Multicultural Education

Despite an overwhelming amount of evidence and research, many believe racial inequality is a social issue of the past and does not currently exist in contemporary America. Multicultural and colorblind approaches to education have, in many ways, allowed these same beliefs to persist throughout schools, placing minority students in a precarious situation where their quality of education is compromised because of schools' inability to recognize the need for racial equity. One of education's earliest responses to racial inequality seen in schools across the nation was multiculturalism. As a form of curriculum reform, multiculturalism was introduced into K-12 education as means of sensitizing "individuals toward ethnic and racial differences, and to increase individual awareness of cultural traditions and sociological experiences" (Mattai, 1992, p. 66). In discussing multiculturalism, Banks (1986) argued that a multicultural education provides an integration of diverse perspectives across various components of school, such as teaching practices, materials, and programs that theoretically could lead to educational equality for students of all races. In theory, multicultural education values cultural pluralism and believes that racial, ethnic, and cultural diversity should not only be valued, but also be embedded within the fabric of education institutions (Mattai, 1992).

Multicultural Literature

Much like multicultural education broadly speaking, multicultural literature derived as a political response to issues of inequality throughout larger society (Cai & Sims Bishop, 1994). Prior to multicultural education and literature, the experiences of people of color were either non-existent or culturally or historically inaccurate, denying students of color opportunities to read texts that offered a counter story to dominant narratives that misrepresented their stories (Hughes-Hassell, Barkley, & Koehler, 2009). Exclusion of minority voices from within the literary canon, particularly as a curricular approach, not only sends a message to students of color that their experiences and stories are not important, it also reinforces the world view that white, heteronormative voices are "truth" and "real history" (Ladson-Billings, 2002). If we are to, as Ladson-Billings (2002) states, provide voice to marginalized groups in hopes of communicating the experiences and realities of those who are oppressed, the stories of people of color must be brought to the forefront of literary work. Such ideologies that promoted the celebration of diverse cultures as a form of global citizenship development and valid educational knowledge gave rise to global (international) literature within American schools.

Global literature, while recognizing and giving voice to authors and stories from diverse racial, cultural and ethnic backgrounds, also considers a more global perspective that includes literary works that represent other countries, regions, and global populations, such as pan-indigenous peoples: Native Americans, First Nations, Inuit, Aboriginal, Maori, Sami, etc. (Bean, Dunkerly-Bean, & Harper, 2017). As an educational tool, literature that spans across the globe and various cultures and nationalities allows teachers and educators to help students adopt a global perspective (Buck et al., 2011). While multicultural and global literature allowed for new opportunities and voices in literature, there was a great deal of resistance. While some viewed multicultural and global literature as a necessity, particularly for the educational benefit of minority students, others with more conservative ideologies viewed multiculturalism as a direct threat to Western culture (Taxel, 1997). As students learned more about other cultures and ethnicities, those resistant to cultural diversity viewed multicultural education, and in particular, "multicultural literature as a threat to the very fabric of Western Civilization" (Taxel, 1997. p. 417).

Even without resistance from those opposed to cultural pluralism, multicultural education, and multicultural literature by extension, would never be able to achieve the aim of eradicating racial inequity within education, nor would it ever provide space within classroom discussion for critical conversations about racism. Education as a field is more reflective of a colorblind approach (Bonilla-Silva, 2005). As Ladson-Billings (1998) contends, education in the United States has a history of ignoring issues of race and racism in favor of idyllic notions of racial harmony. Furthermore, despite years of research that prove otherwise, many within education like to believe that issues of racial inequality experience throughout society do not manifest within schools. Beliefs such as these make it difficult, if not possible, to address racial disparities that impact marginalized students because concerns like academic achievement, and school discipline, for example, are not evaluated within the context of race. Mattai (1992) argues that multicultural education is largely unsuccessful at addressing race and racism because it does not specifically center race nor offer any teaching strategies to do so. Furthermore, multicultural education and its implementation within ELA classes are void of institutional support and community, rendering any work done around racial justice merely symbolic (Mattai, 1992). The inability of multicultural education to effectively be used as an agent of change for anti-racist teaching practices makes it nearly impossible for meaningful anti-racist work to be done within classrooms.

As multicultural education has shown, "traditional approaches to democratic education conceive racism in terms of personal prejudice, they cannot adequately address the problems that racism actually poses" (Thompson, 1997, p. 7). That is, teachers and teacher educators cannot rely on cultural celebratory practices alone to try and begin undoing the destruction years of systemic racism has created. As teachers move beyond multicultural education, it is imperative for them to adopt anti-racist teaching pedagogies that center racism and examine the role of race in inequalities seen both in and out of school. Unlike multicultural education, which looks across multiple cultural and ethnic groups without specifically considering race and systems of racism, anti-racist teaching offers a concerted engagement with work focused on ending racism (Gupta, 2003), even as it intersects with different identities (Crenshaw, 1989 and 1991) seen throughout classrooms.

Anti-racist Pedagogy

As it relates particularly to Black and minority students who are historically marginalized within their everyday lives and then again while in school, anti-racist pedagogy is an absolute necessity for their academic success. Anti-racist pedagogy, unlike multicultural education, is more effective at addressing racial biases because it critiques education policies and practices that, under multicultural education, "operate beneath a veneer of professed tolerance and diversity" (Gillborn, 2006, p. 11). More importantly, anti-racist teaching includes structural, rather than individual, analysis to understand race's impact on students (Godreau & Llorens, 2010). For teachers and educators, a structural analysis of educational racism requires a critical examination of existing means of assessment and testing, curriculum, teacher education, and school disciplinary practices (Gillborn, 2006; Godreau & Llorens, 2010). For ELA teachers, calls for anti-racist pedagogy require teachers to condemn practices such as eurocentric and one-dimensional definition of literacy and literacy practices or classroom libraries that fail to promote readership of diverse perspectives and experiences. Anti-racist literacy education must, for example, move beyond the cannon and implement contemporary voices of color as texts used to discuss systemic and historical racism and do so within a contemporary context that leads to meaningful discussion about race and racism for students (Worlds & Miller, 2019). Critical race theory (CRT), then, represents not just a foundational theory for understanding race, but also a conceptual framework to guide one's understanding of how to approach anti-racist teaching.

Theoretical Framework

Critical race theory (CRT), which emerged from critical legal studies, is an epistemology that focuses specifically on race and racism in the United States legal system (Tate, 1997; Delgado & Stefanic, 2001). While other theories and epistemologies consider various components, such as socio-economic status/class, gender, and sexuality, critical race theorists prioritize race as a primary factor and seek to understand how race impacts intersecting identities (Crenshaw, 2011). Despite its roots in legal studies, critical race theory has evolved into a multidisciplinary theory (Hughes-Hassell, Barkley, & Koehler, 2009) that scholars and researchers across a diverse range of academic disciplines use. Within the context of educational research studies, scholars have widely considered a number of factors when examining various issues in education. However, more scholars have recognized the need to understand the role race and racism has on a number of problems that plague the education system. Understanding that the tangible impacts that racism has that are seen throughout society at large also impact and shape schools and student learning (Ladson-Billings & Tate, 1995), education scholars have examined the many areas of education that are shaped by race and racism, including curriculum (Ladson-Billings, 1998), school funding (Aleman, 2007), and school discipline policies (Dixson, 2006). While CRT has created space for discourse around systemic racism in schools, scholars have also noted the power of CRT to help teachers discuss race and racism with students.

Many educators, particularly English Language Arts teachers, have found critical race theory a compellingly useful framework and tool to use specifically within their ELA classrooms. Given CRTs' explicit focus on the significance of race and racism, it comes as no surprise that a theory with origins in the field of legal studies has crossed disciplinary boundaries and has developed footing in academic content specific conversations. As teachers utilize CRT to understand institutional racism throughout society, CRT also provides language and framework for teachers to have serious discussions about race and racism within the context of content related conversations. In particular, specific literary genres such as young adult literature that explore issues of racial discrimination and inequity lends itself very well to classroom and group discussions using critical race theory. Young adult literature that shares Black character's experiences with racism, in general, has followed a thematic tradition that includes discussion of race and racism. Additionally, many of these literary works have used tenets of critical race theory to not only challenge representations of Black life in America and abroad, but also give voice to historically marginalized groups whose work and words have been silenced by exclusive and hegemonic literary canon (Bishop, 2007; Harris, 1997).

CRT as an application enables a foregrounding of racial issues (Brooks, 2006, p. 42) that allows intentional exploration of race within a number of literary texts used in Language Arts classrooms. Furthermore, it is a critical lens that serves as a tool for literary analysis that "enables researchers, teachers, teacher-educators as well as youth to systematically understand some of racism's enduring influence" (p. 42). Because of YA's wide use within language arts curricula, there is an enormous danger present when students are asked to make meaning of the text without strongly considering race. As educators, we deny students of the opportunity for rich and meaningful discussions about race within the classroom when we fail to ask them to consider the ways in which race impacts the world they live in. CRT allows open and honest conversations where students are able to speak frankly about the impact racism has had on society. Frank conversations about racism can too easily be avoided if we ask students to rely solely on literary theories that do not explicitly address race. The need for understanding the role of racism in American institutions like education and actively fighting against it reflects the tenets of culturally relevant pedagogy that many scholars argue is important for students (Ladson-Billings, 1995; Ladson-Billings & Tate, 1995), particularly students of color. CRT allows opportunities for close readings of historical fiction and other literary works that centralize race and builds on existing reader response theories that have typically been suggested for students. Critical race theory asks students, both Black and white, to draw on their own experiences with racism and use that personal background knowledge to contextualize their understanding of young adult texts that centralize race.

The Books

In this section, we provide examples of young adult literature that can be used as a vehicle for facilitating discussions on race and racism toward the development of anti-racist pedagogy (Gillborn, 2006; Ladson-Billings & Tate, 1995). While each text offers numerous approaches, we've organized the books according to a central theme that anchors each text in contemporary socio-political issues. These books, which present identities and experiences by and about Black, Indigenous, and People of Color (BIPOC), allow students to converse about race and racism through a global perspective that recognizes various cultures and nationalities (Buck et al., 2011).

On Police Brutality

As countless police officers continue to enforce anti-Black racism through the senseless murdering of Black people, the discussion of racist police violence and police brutality is both timely and necessary. While nonfiction texts such as podcasts, articles, and documentaries can be powerful ways to facilitate discussions on current issues of police brutality, young adult literature can be sites to critically analyze and problematize fictional spaces reminiscent of our lived reality. The suggested novels are summarized below:

How It Went Down by Kekla Magoon (2014)
    Sixteen-year-old Tariq Johnson dies from two gunshot wounds, and the story varies from the witnesses, the community, and the shooter himself. While individuals struggle to describe how his murder went down, an uproar occurs as people argue over how Tariq should be remembered and who is to blame for his death.

The Hate U Give by Angie Thomas (2017)
    Starr Carter is a sixteen-year-old caught between two identities—who she is in her poor neighborhood and who she becomes at her elite prep school. After a party one night, Starr witnesses a police officer murder her childhood

best friend, Khalil. As protests begin, Starr must choose who and what she believes.

All American Boys by Jason Reynolds and Brendan Kiely (2015)

Two classmates, Rashad and Quinn, struggle to find common ground after Rashad was brutally beaten by a police officer who wrongly suspected him of stealing and assaulting a white woman. After a video of the encounter goes viral, Quinn must decide to act on what he witnessed or continue his silence on racial profiling and police brutality.

Dear Martin by Nic Stone (2017)

While Justyce grapples with modern day racial injustices by writing letters to historical civil rights leader Dr. Martin Luther King Jr., he becomes the center of conversations on police brutality after Justyce and his friend Manny are approached by a group of white police officers. After shots are fired, Justyce faces criticism from the media and his community.

On Mass Incarceration

Like police brutality, mass incarceration is a systemic issue that unequivocally harms people of color as a result of over-policing and policies rooted in racism. The criminal justice system in America is anything but fair. Accordingly, chances are that incarceration has impacted the families and communities surrounding your classroom. Conversations around the jail and prison system are especially relevant for today's youth, as arguments to defund police and reform the criminal justice system attempt to combat racial disparities in our society. The suggested novels are summarized below:

Miles Morales: Spider-Man by Jason Reynolds (2017)

Miles, a teenager who was recently suspended from school, begins to question his many identities: Black, Puerto Rican, and Spider-Man. In addition to saving people's lives, Miles has to navigate racism and poverty while examining the role of the prison system.

Barely Missing Everything by Matt Mendez (2019)

Juan and JD embark on a cross country journey to meet Mando-- a man on death row claiming to be Juan's supposedly dead father. While the two teenagers can't wait to leave their hometowns behind, their adventure reminds them of the continuing racial injustices facing people of color.

On Bullying

Although many people experience bullying, Black, Indigenous, and people of color (BIPOC) often encounter harassment explicitly tied to their race or ethnicity. Stories about bullying, especially bullying tied to racism, can be helpful for building an anti-racist classroom that both names and condemns community standards that dehumanize others. The suggested novels are summarized below:

Here to Stay by Sara Farizan (2018)

When Bijan unexpectedly leads his varsity basketball team to victory, people start to take notice of him. Once a shy student on the sideline, Bijan rises in popularity while also experiencing Islamophobia by his teammates after a photo circulates of him depicted as a terrorist. Even though he has a supportive community, Bijan grapples with speaking up against prejudice.

A Very Large Expanse of Sea by Tahereh Mafi (2019)

When Shirin begins attending a new high school, she is bullied in part because of her Muslim identity, as her classmates ignorantly associate her with terrorism post-9/11. While Shirin's decision to wear a headscarf leads to racist harassment, she questions how to respond.

Felix Ever After by Kacen Callender (2020)

Even though it's summer, Felix and his classmates are preparing for senior year by attending an art program hosted by their high school. When someone creates a photo gallery containing old pictures of Felix and begins harassing him online, Felix questions why his existence as a Black, transgender boy seems to invite harassment.

Representation Matters

Many, including YAL author Nic Stone (2020), have made arguments for reading books about Black people living in addition to stories about racism and other socio-political issues. While this chapter is about utilizing young adult literature to discuss race and racism as part of an anti-racist pedagogy, we acknowledge that representations of blackness beyond characters experiencing oppression as a result of racism are also critical to developing students' understanding of Black people. Providing students with reading experiences that center BIPOC characters and their stories outside of racial inequality is a necessary step for working toward anti-racist teaching. We give a brief list of recommended texts below toward this suggestion:

- *Clap When You Land* by Elizabeth Acevedo (2020)
- *Children of Blood and Bone* by Tomi Adeyemi (2018)
- *To All the Boys I've Loved Before* by Jenny Han (2014)
- *You Should See Me in a Crown* by Leah Johnson (2020)
- *The Astonishing Color of After* by Emily X.R. Pan (2018)
- *Gabi, a Girl in Pieces* by Isabel Quintero (2014)
- *Odd One Out* by Nic Stone (2018)
- *The Sun Is Also a Star* by Nicola Yoon (2016)

Classroom Application

There is an emerging body of scholarship discussing possibilities for utilizing young adult literature as a vehicle for discussing socio-political issues such as race and racism with students (Boyd, 2017; Glasgow, 2001; Schieble, 2012; Thomas, 2019; Worlds & Miller, 2019). While we trust teachers to make pedagogical decisions that best fit the needs of their students, we discuss a few ideas below for facilitating conversations around race and racism.

Silent Discussion

While the silent discussion (also known as Chalk Talk, among other names) can be used at any point during a unit of study, we like to begin a unit by posing essential questions that might inform our thinking at the beginning of a novel study. Using chart paper or other material options that allow for space for collaborative writing, write down an open-ended question that would solicit varying opinions. Depending on the size of your group, you will want to have multiple pieces of chart paper with a variety of discussion questions. For example, in a unit exploring police brutality using the novel *How It Went Down* by Kekla Magoon (2014), we might use the question "How does a person's identity influence their perspective?" After writing down one question per piece of chart paper, students will participate in the discussion by visiting each piece of paper and responding by writing on the chart paper. Depending on your purpose, responses can be anonymous, or students can sign their names. You should also encourage students to build on or challenge others' responses on the chart paper. The only real rule for this activity is that it should be silent. The responses can then be used to facilitate conversations as you begin reading. We've also used silent discussions to track how ideas change during a unit (e.g. silent discussions with the same questions prior to beginning and after ending a novel).

Critical Viewfinder

In a camera, the viewfinder shows the field of view of the lens, which frames and focuses an image prior to taking a piece. In this activity, students perceive the text and the world around them through a critical lens, paying special attention to how race and racism might be constructed in various ways. During a unit discussing bullying alongside the novel *Felix Ever After* by Kacen Callender (2020), students could choose short excerpts of the text displaying moments of bullying from a provided list. Within their chosen excerpt, students could begin by answering broad questions like, "What do you notice? What do you wonder?" After initial thoughts about their excerpt, students could examine how race is discussed in the excerpt. This activity could be paired with critical examinations of other texts featuring bullying, such as song lyrics or advertisements with similar analysis questions.

Visual Exploration Project

For this activity, students can work individually or within a group to display their understanding of race and racism based on a unit of study using visuals. They might decide to investigate localized issues of racism in their community or interests rooted in their personal experiences or out of school literacy lives (e.g. critically examining other texts like T.V. shows, movies, podcasts, etc.). For example, during a study of mass incarceration using the novel *Barely Missing Everything* by Matt Mendez (2019) and other supplemental resources, students might decide to research the juvenile prison system in their own community or how incarceration is discussed in the local media. Based on their research, their project can be created using various virtual mediums or non-virtual methods that use visuals to explain their findings. Students can present their projects to their peers through a traditional presentation or museum walk, drawing further wonderings about race and racism as it connects to other projects and their own lives.

Conclusion

While progression in terms of race relations and racial equity appear unpromising in the near future, practicing and future teachers have a growing amount of scholarship on anti-racist pedagogy to turn to. Efforts to implement anti-racist teaching throughout curriculum will continue to be met with much resistance. However, teachers, particularly ELA instructors, have the power to create learning spaces that promote equity and justice. As teachers consider how they might cultivate equitable environments that are just, it is imperative that educators themselves be committed to anti-racism. Stakes are far too high for students to learn from teachers who simply disagree with racism. True freedom for many of our most vulnerable student populations ask that teachers actively seek ways to be anti-racist. Course syllabi represent an excellent starting place to incorporate anti-racism. Racial inequality that students experience outside of classrooms is exacerbated when the curriculum through which students attempt to learn is inherently racist. As such, educators can review their course materials and identify areas that lack representation and begin to add more diverse perspectives. For example, the growing availability of diverse young adult literature has allowed ELA teachers new opportunities to provide literature engagement that speaks toward historically marginalized voices. By challenging traditional sources of knowledge and including otherwise excluded voices, teachers can begin to center the perspectives of people who are most impacted by racism. Teachers can also reimagine how learning is assessed and include assessment that accepts various cultural learning styles as valid and utilizes cultural funds of knowledge as legitimate knowledge sources. Intentional changes like these reject traditional perspectives of education that miseducate students, teaching them that true learning cannot exist outside of an anglocentric conceptualization of what it means to learn.

Racial inequity remains one of the most harmful sins whose impact on the lives of Black and minority people have proven detrimental, if not deadly. Moreover, racism's direct impact on the lives of children is routinely and systematically manifested in the quality of education that students from historically marginalized communities receive. As the racial climate within the United States and abroad continues to grow more hostile toward Black, Indigenous, and other people of color (BIPOC), teachers, now more than ever, must be committed to anti-racist teaching. The responsibility of providing educational experiences that attend to students' academic needs cannot be met in its entirety if learning occurs outside of an instructional framework that is grounded in anti-racist pedagogy. While many educators and scholars have previously turned to multicultural education and multicultural literature to address racial inequality, the current socio-political climate demands that teachers currently in and entering the field explicitly address racism and racial inequality through their own teaching. Ongoing disparities in academic achievement along racial and socio-economic lines have starkly revealed the limitations of a multicultural approach to education. Thus, teaching practices must include more intentional efforts to promote a liberatory education that allows students opportunities to learn academic skills and contents used to help them challenge the status quo.

Discussion Questions

1. Select a YA text either from your personal collection or one suggested by the authors. Consider the approaches presented by the authors to facilitate conversations around race and racism (Silent Discussion, Critical Viewfinder, Visual Exploration Project). How can you implement these approaches to engage in critical conversations?
2. What other instructional approaches might you use to engage in anti-racist teaching with YA literature?

Literature Cited

Acevedo, E. (2020). *Clap when you land*. Quill Tree Books.

Adeyemi, T. (2018). *Children of blood and bone*. Henry Holt and Company.

Callender, K. (2020). *Felix ever after*. HarperCollins.

Farizan, S. (2018). *Here to stay*. Algonquin Young Readers.

Han, J. (2014). *To all the boys I've loved before*. Simon & Schuster Books for Young Readers.

Johnson, K. (2020). *You should see me in a crown*. Scholastic Press.

Mafi, T. (2019). *A very large expanse of sea*. HarperCollins.

Magoon, K. (2014). *How it went down*. Henry Holt and Company.

Mendez, M. (2019). *Barely missing everything*. Atheneum/Caitlyn Dlouhy Books.

Pan, E. X. R. (2018). *The astonishing color of after*. Little, Brown Books for Young Readers.

Quintero, I. (2014). *Gabi, a girl in pieces*. Cinco Puntos Press.

Reynolds, J. (2017). *Miles morales: Spider-man*. Marvel Press.

Reynolds, J., & Kiely, B. (2015). *All American boys*. Atheneum/Caitlyn Dlouhy Books.

Stone, N. (2017). *Dear Martin*. Crown.

Stone, N. (2018). *Odd one out*. Crown.

Thomas, A. (2017). *The hate u give*. Balzer + Bray.

Yoon, N. (2016). *The sun is also a star*. Ember.

References

Alemán, E. (2007). Situating Texas school finance policy in a CRT framework: How "substantially equal" yields racial inequity. *Educational Administration Quarterly*, *43* (5), 525--558.

Banks, J. A. (1986). Multiethnic education and its critics: Britain and the United States. In S. Modgil, G. K. Verma, K. Mallick, & C. Modgil (Eds.), *Multicultural education: The interminable debate* (pp. 221–232). London: Falmer Press.

Bean, T., Dunkerly-Bean, J., Harper, H. (2017). *Teaching young adults literature: Developing students as world citizens.* Thousand Oaks, CA: SAGE Publishing, Ltd.

Bell, D. (1995). Who's afraid of critical race theory?" *University of Illinois Law Review, 95*(4), 893–910.

Bishop, R. S. (2007). *Free within ourselves: The development of African American children's literature.* Westport, CT: Greenwood P.

Bonilla-Silva, E. (2003). *Racism without racists: Color-blind racism and the persistence of racial inequality In the United States.* Lanham, MD: Rowman & Littlefield.

Boyd, A. S. (2017). *Social justice literacies in the English classroom: Teaching practice in action.* Teachers College Press.

Brooks, W. (2006). Reading representations of themselves: Urban youth use culture and African American textual features to develop literary understandings. *Reading Research Quarterly, 4*(3), 372–392.

Buck, C., Gilrane, C., Brown, C., Hendricks, D., Rearden, K., & Wilson, N. (2011). There's hope in the story: Learning culture through international and intercultural children's and young adult literature. *New England Reading Association Journal, 47*(1), 49.

Cai, M. & Sims Bishop, R. (1994). Multicultural literature for children: Towards a clarification of the concept. In A. Haas Dyson and C. Genishi (Eds.), *The Need for Story: Cultural Diversity in Classroom and Community.* National Council of Teachers of English.

Crenshaw, K. (1989). Demarginalizing the intersection of race and sex: A Black Feminist critique of antidiscrimination doctrine, Feminist Theory and Antiracist Politics.U.Chi.Legal F., 1989 – HeinOnline.

Crenshaw, K. (1991). Mapping the margins: Intersectionality, identity politics, and violence against women of color. *Stanford Law Review, 43*(6), 1241–1299.

Crenshaw, K. W. (2011). Twenty years of critical race theory: Looking back to move forward. *Connecticut Law Review, 43*(5), 1256–1300.

Delgado, R. (1995). *Critical race theory: The cutting edge.* Philadelphia: Temple University Press.

Delgado, R. & Stefanic, J. (2001). *Critical race theory: An introduction.* New York: New York University.

Dixson, A. D. (2006). The fire this time: Jazz, research and critical race theory. In A. D. Dixson & C. K. Rousseau (Eds.), *Critical race theory in education* (pp. 213–230). New York: Routledge.

Gillborn, D. (2006). Critical race theory and education: Racism and anti-racism in educational theory and praxis. *Discourse: Studies in the Cultural Politics of Education, 27*(1), 11–32.

Glasgow, J. N. (2001). Teaching social justice through young adult literature. *The English Journal, 90*(6), 54–61.

Godreau, I. P., & Llorens, H. (2010). Pulling up myths from the root: Designing and implementing an anti-racist curriculum about the African heritage for third graders in Puerto Rico. *Practicing Anthropology, 32*(1), 26–31.

Gupta, T. D. (2003). Teaching anti-racist research in the academy. *Teaching Sociology, 31*(4), 456–468.

Harris, V. J. (1997). *Children's literature depicting blacks: Using multiethnic literature in the K-8 classroom.* Ed. V. Harris. Norwood, MA: Christopher Gordon.

Hughes-Hassell, S., Barkley, H. A., & Koehler, E. (2009). Promoting equity in children's literacy instruction: Using a critical race theory framework to examine transitional books. *Research Journal of the American Association of School Librarians, 12*(1), 1–20.

Johnson, H., Mathis, J., & Short, K. G. (2017). *Critical content analysis of children's and young adult literature: Reframing perspectives.* New York, NY: Routledge.

Ladson-Billings, G., & Tate, W. (1995). Toward a critical race theory of education. *Teachers College Record, 97*(1), 47–69.

Ladson-Billings, G. (1998). Just what is critical race theory and what's it doing in a nice field like education. *International Journal of Qualitative Studies in Education, 11*(1), 7–24.

Ladson-Billings, G. (2002). But that's just good teaching! the case for culturally relevant pedagogy. In S. J. Denbo & L. M. Beaulieu (Eds.), *Improving schools for African American students: A reader for educational leaders* (pp. 95–102). Charles C Thomas Publisher, Ltd.

Freire, P. (1972). *Cultural action for freedom.* Harmondsworth, UK: Penguin.

Freire, P. (1984). *Pedagogy of the oppressed.* New York: Continuum.

Freire, P., & Macedo, D. P. (1987). *Literacy: Reading the word & the world.* South Hadley, MA: Bergin & Garvey Publishers.

Mattai, P. R. (1992). Rethinking the nature of multicultural education: Has it lost its focus or is it being misused? *Journal of Negro Education, 61*(1), 65–77.

Mayo, P. (1999). *Gramsci, Freire, and adult education: Possibilities for transformative action.* London: Zed Books.

Schieble, M. (2012). Critical conversations on whiteness with young adult literature. *Journal of Adolescent & Adult Literacy, 56*(3), 212–221.

Stone, N. (2020, June 08). Don't just read about racism: Read stories about black people living. Retrieved from https://www.cosmopolitan.com/entertainment/books/a32770951/read-black-books-nic-stone/

Tator, C., & F. Henry. (1991). *Multicultural education: Translating policy into practice.* Ottawa: Multiculturalism and Citizenship Canada.

Taxel, J. (1997). Multicultural literature and the politics of reaction. *Teacher's College Record, 98, 417-448.*

Taxel, J. (2007). Reading multicultural children's literature: Response, resistance, and reflection. *Teaching in Translation, 17*(2), 106–116.

Thomas, E. E. (2019). *The dark fantastic: Race and the imagination from Harry Potter to The Hunger Games.* NYU Press.

Thompson, A. (1997). For: Anti-racist education. *Curriculum Inquiry, 27*(1), 7–44.

Troyna, B. (2006). Beyond multiculturalism: Towards the enactment of anti-racist education in policy, provision and pedagogy. *Oxford Review of Education, 13*(3), 307–320.

Worlds, M., & Miller, C. (2019). Miles Morales: Spider-Man and reimagining the canon for racial justice. *English Journal, 4*(108), 43–50.

8. Empowering Students to Engage in Global Children's and Young Adult Literature Through Multimodal Practices Using Instructional Technology

Janeen M. Pizzo & Logan Rath

Students in a sixth grade ELA block are reading Padma Venkatraman's middle grade novel, *The Bridge Home*. Students immediately connect with the main characters and are naturally curious to learn about India, where the novel is set. To prepare for this lesson, the teacher shares on social media that she's reading *The Bridge Home* with her classes and asks if teachers in her Professional Learning Network (PLN), an online professional community, want to connect. Within two hours she and a colleague in another region create a digital partnership. Throughout the novel study, students are crafting their own questions, talking to their partner class via FlipGrid, a website where students can leave video comments for each other, or Skype, a video conferencing software, and engaging in digital double-entry journals, making collaboration with their physically-distant groupmates easy. Using Google Earth, a virtual field trip software, they travel to India and visit settings in the book. At the conclusion of the read, students are given similar choices for their final projects. Some students share memes through their class's social media page that include thoughtful captions behind the meme. Others pitch alternate endings, and work in groups to co-construct a new final chapter in both audio and text. A third group acts out their favorite scenes, recording a movie and splicing together recordings made in different physical locations. At the end, students reflect on their experiences with the unit and celebrate their new understandings with each other.

This teacher took advantage of multimodal learning approaches to connect her students to the world around them through 21ˢᵗ century collaboration. As authors with extensive experience integrating multimodality into the classroom setting, we argue that this approach enhances student learning and engages students with globally-connected, authentic learning experiences that are only possible through the use of technology (Puentedura, 2015). For the purposes of this chapter, we explore how multimodal approaches work well with children's and young adult literature.

Global children's and young adult literature are gateways to facilitating awareness and activism. When students read stories with characters who are like them, they may feel validated and connected to the classroom (Paris & Alim, 2017). When they read novels that have characters from different backgrounds, children can develop empathy and understanding about humanity. Misconceptions and cultural assumptions can be challenged through literature and help students to recognize their own biases (McNair, 2016).

Multimodality Through Technology

Throughout this chapter, we operate from the conceptual framework of multimodality through technology due to our own experiences in this area. Janeen is a cisgender white female with years of experience working with technology in the K-12 setting as an English teacher and literacy specialist. Logan is a cisgender white male who studied Spanish education and is currently a librarian supporting education professors and teaching about technology integration in K-12. We bring these experiences and our positionality to the discussion.

Multimodality is the simultaneous use of more than one mode to communicate meaning. Specific modes include language, sound, visuals, gestures, and space or layout. Each of these modes have their own benefits and limitations (Jewitt, 2009). For example, music can be experienced either through sound or through the visual/spatial combination that is sheet music. Each mode is used purposefully, and requires different resources to bring them to life. Multiliteracies are the socially, culturally, and textually based practices required to communicate and make meaning using different modalities (Serafini & Gee, 2017). While multiliteracies and multimodality are related, they are not synonymous.

Young children and English language learners use multimodality to decode the English language before they are able to understand the written word (Takacs & Bus, 2018). In schools, children experience multimodality all the time, especially when using technology. Unfortunately, schools tend to privilege the linguistic mode as if it is the only way to make meaning (Rowsell, 2013). Shifting to multimodal approaches for assignments allows for students who are not particularly strong in responding through writing to demonstrate their comprehension. It is our hope that this chapter will demonstrate how to incorporate technology alongside global children's and young adult literature so that teachers can bring multimodal responses to their classroom in culturally relevant ways.

What are multimodal learning experiences?

Walking into a classroom that supports students' learning through multimodal approaches through technology, one is likely to find students talking with each other and engaging in online collaboration with students from another state. For example, students will have access to microphones and other technology, enabling them to have innovative ways to express their learning. There will be a lot going on and that's the point! As Taylor and Leung (2020) highlight, "literacy is multimodal" (p. 1). When students engage in learning, they naturally engage in multimodality (Dalton, 2012; Kress, 2003; Kress & van Leeuwen, 2001). They engage in conversations with each other complete with nonverbal gestures, they listen to podcasts, watch videos, and take ownership of their learning environment, all of which support the "linguistic, visual, audio, gestural, and spatial elements" of learning (Dalton, 2012; Cope & Kalantzis, 2009). As Boyd and Tochelli (2014) stated, "For today's students - those who have never known a world without multiple modes for meaning making - multimodality is central to their everyday lives" (p. 292). So, what is a multimodal learning experience? It requires providing a variety of choices for students to demonstrate their learning; whether through verbal, visual, gestural or any combination of modes. These experiences honor students' strengths, can push them out of their comfort zones, and add life to the classroom. Multimodality can help teachers work with students to express their own identities through the choices in a given project. Students have access to so many forms of receiving and sharing new information. As a result, when it comes to considering text we believe that experiencing global children's literature through one mode would be a significant disservice to our students.

Opportunities for Multimodal Learning Through Technology

The teacher in the opening of this chapter provided students with choices and employed technology to offer interactive components to the novel study. The novel study utilized multiple strategies, processes, and experiences that had the potential to positively influence long-term learning (Fisher et al., 2016). When engaging in multimodal learning with novels it is important for teachers to incorporate the International Society for Technology in Education (ISTE) (2020) standards that support student-centered learning, take advantage of the SAMR (Substitution, Augmentation, Modification, Redefinition) model (Puentedura, 2015) to design appropriate instances of technology integration, and learn how technology, pedagogy and content interact by studying the Technological Pedagogical Content Knowledge, or TPACK framework (Koehler & Mishra, 2009). We discuss the ISTE standards, SAMR models, and TPACK framework below.

TPACK Framework

The TPACK framework for successful technology integration in the classroom is useful for understanding the various skills teachers need to incorporate technology into a specific educational context (Koehler & Mishra, 2009). TPACK explores the intersections of technology, content, and pedagogy by considering the following questions during planning:

Technical Content Knowledge (TCK)

- How does technology affect the delivery of content?
- Which technologies are best for a specific content area?·

Pedagogical Content Knowledge (PCK)

- How can the content be presented in a way for others to understand it?
- Which teaching methods work for a particular discipline?

Technological Pedagogical Knowledge (TPK)

- How does technology affect teaching practices?
- How can technology lead to more student-centered learning?

The questions above help teachers anchor technology use with instructional planning. Understanding how pedagogy, technology, and content are connected will allow teachers to make decisions that positively and effectively impact student performance in the classroom.

SAMR Model

The Substitution, Augmentation, Modification, and Redefinition (SAMR) model was created by Dr. Ruben R. Puentedura in 2013 as a way to help teachers identify and evaluate their integration of instructional technology in their classrooms. The SAMR model provides a framework that shows teachers where they are on a scale in their implementation of instructional technology. This knowledge can invigorate teachers; encouraging them to make adjustments to their instruction to move beyond basic levels of technology use in their classroom. Each component of SAMR is described below highlighting its potential use during the novel study of *Darius the Great is Not Okay* by Adib Khorram. This award-winning novel follows the story of Darius Kellner, a young man dealing with depression, his own identity, and his trip to Iran where he visits his mother's family.

Substitution: Technology acts as a direct substitute with no functional change.

- *Example*: Reading an e-book version of the novel *Darius the Great is Not Okay*.
- *Explanation:* The e-book substitutes the paper copy of the novel which can be read on students' devices. The task of reading the novel doesn't change thus technology is just a direct substitute.

Augmentation: Technology acts as a direct tool substitute, with functional improvement.

- *Example*: As students enjoy traveling to Iran with Darius, they use the internet to locate information on topics they are curious about while reading such as Persian culture, Farsi, teen depression, etc.
- *Explanation*: This activity allows students to drive the learning. Traditionally, students would view a teacher-prepared slideshow periodically that would give them the information on major components of novels. Now, with the use of technology, students can answer the questions *they* are curious about while they read, not what the teacher thinks they should be curious about. They can then share with their classmates their learning.

Modification: Technology allows for significant task redesign.

- *Example*: Students work in literature groups to collaboratively write in a shared online space collecting important quotes, highlighting events/scenes from the novel, sharing connections they are making, and asking each other questions. They have choices in recording their conversations via the Synth podcast tool, creating videos, or simply using Google Docs or Office365.
- *Explanation*: Students not only have the opportunity to work together on a collaborative document, but they have access to their choice of learning modality. With technology this task is significantly redesigned from a series of paper worksheets to something students can co-create and it's digital which means anyone, with permission, can access the work and provide feedback.

Redefinition: Technology allows for the creation of new tasks, previously inconceivable.

- *Example*: A class from rural Hilton, New York connects with a classroom from Arlington, Virginia. They read the book in their classes, but regularly connect with each other via FlipGrid or Skype and share their insights on the novel. They build their own reading book club across state lines and work together to create projects based on investigative topics of student interest like mental health awareness, Persian culture, Iranian football, architecture of Iran, basic Farsi, and the unfamiliar teas introduced in the novel. Collectively, students realize that the world is much larger than their school; this helps develop intercultural understandings.
- *Explanation*: Learning at this stage is enhanced by technology and affords students unique learning experiences. It allows novels to come to life through digital discourse, inquiry, and online travel.

Please note, while the SAMR model looks like it represents a hierarchy starting with Redefinition being the ideal instructional goal, that is not the intended use of SAMR. The model is meant to give educators a chance to rethink how to approach curriculum, and asks teachers to consider the possibilities of making adjustments to go beyond basic uses of technology.

Suggestions for Teachers

Teachers can integrate different types of multimodal practices into their classrooms when engaging in novel study. We emphasize that technology changes rapidly. To assist with app selection, we rely upon the website Common Sense's EdTech Reviews to stay current.

Digital Book Creation

What is it?

Digital book creation goes beyond the standard creation of a picture book that would combine pictures and text. Digital books can be static or interactive, combining video, text and sound. Use of Book Creator has been shown to engage students with literacy practices and to give agency to students who were otherwise deemed struggling in the classroom (Tavernier, 2016).

Tools for Creating Digital Books

Book Creator (http://www.bookcreator.com) is a popular resource for creating digital books. This app allows students to bring together visuals (drawings, photos, video), sound, and written text to bring a story to life. Additionally, iBooks Author, PowerPoint/Google Slides, Microsoft Sway, and Storybird all allow for digital book creation.

Examples of Multimodal Learning Through Digital Book Creation

Creating digital books in your classroom can take many forms such as visual retellings of folktales or beliefs of a given culture, collaborative guides about a region or country, and multimodal glossaries from a novel. Having students create nonfiction digital books that synthesizes new learning is one way to incorporate digital books into the classroom.

Project idea. We suggest teachers use the celebrated coming of age LGBTQ+ YA novel, *Aristotle and Dante Discover the Secrets of the Universe* by Benjamin Alire Sáenz. In each of the six sections of this novel, there is an opening epigraph. Have students choose one of the epigraphs and create a page for a class book that demonstrates their new learning, understanding or connection to the real-life implications behind the novel's themes.

Considerations for digital book creation. When creating a digital book, like any other story, it is important to consider the writing process. Outlining and drafting your story before engaging with the app will set students up for success. Web-based digital book creator software often requires a consistent connection to the internet whereas standalone software does not.

Podcasting

What is it?

Podcasts, which are essentially audio files (such as. mp3 or. wav), allow for students to completely abandon the published written word and tell the story through voice. Any device with a microphone such as an iPad, Chromebook, or smartphone, can record voice memos. Podcasts can include students' voices, or they can incorporate background noises, jingles, and audio special effects to add complexity.

Tools for Creating Podcasts

Two free tools to create podcasts are Audacity (https://www.audacityteam. org) and Synth (https://gosynth.com/). These tools allow you to easily record segments, edit sound by combining different tracks, and create class podcasts. Audio tracks containing different recordings are layered together to achieve the final project. Many podcasts often involve hosts who interview different guests each episode. This format would work well for expanding character development or providing an alternative point of view.

Examples of Multimodal Learning Through Podcasts

Podcasts are an effective way to introduce "productive and collaborative talk" which "increases engagement, helps clarify meaning, improves retention of information, shapes and improves thinking capacities, leads to deeper understanding, and results in more enduring learning" (Routman, 2018, pp. 153–154). Podcasting allows conversations to be heard and empowers and validates students' voices.

Project ideas. Combine students' and characters' voices with Character Podcasts. Students can record segments sharing which characters they liked and why, or they can fabricate situations where the characters from the different books meet. For example, using the graphic novel, *Illegal* by Eoin Colfer, older students can combine research on immigration with the experiences shared in the novel. Engaging students in Reflective Podcasts is another way to include podcasts in your classroom. Reading *Stamped: Racism, Antiracism, and You* by Jason Reynolds, students can work to share their new understandings of the racial constructs in America. Additionally, there are Mentor Podcasts. When introducing podcasting as a genre, consider using mentor podcasts as appropriate, such as *Story Seeds, Book Club for Kids*, and NPR's list of podcasts: *Wow in the World, This I Believe,* and *Code Switch.*

Considerations Specific to Podcasts. Podcasts are designed to be shared with outside audiences. When doing this it is important to protect your students' identities and include only first names and last initials and explicitly tell students to remove any identifying information while they are speaking. When recording, it is also important to consider sound and background noise. Microphones are nice to have if the budget allows and podcasts are used regularly, but they are not required.

Video

What is it?
Video projects are often the most daunting for a novice to attempt. However, they are not impossible. The first thing to know about any video project is that it will take much longer than you originally plan. This is mostly due to the editing process when combining various video clips. Video projects can be created by anyone with a camera and microphone.

Tools for Creating Video Projects
While laptops and Chromebooks are not ideal for this task, they can be used if they have a webcam and if other hardware is not available. Digital storytelling is one example of video in a manageable student project. With a digital story, students combine photos with audio (either sound or spoken words), to take advantage of the best of each modality. Digital stories can be produced easily using Movie Maker or iMovie, or even PowerPoint exported as a movie. Adobe Spark, PowToon, and WeVideo are also web-based platforms worth exploring.

Examples of Multimodal Learning Through Video Creation
A common, easy-to-implement use for video is to have students create book trailers, essentially movie trailers for the novels they read. Students read, collect important quotes and themes, engage in the design process to create an appealing trailer and have the satisfaction of being able to share their work with other students. Creating book trailers is an effective way for students to share the books they are reading; generating interest for their peers.

Considerations Specific to Video Creation
When assigning a video project, be sure to have students schedule sufficient time for editing their clips into the final project. Windows Movie Maker and iMovie are free software that run on either Windows or Mac, and allow students to export a movie file. The best advice we can give teachers when choosing where to publish video projects is to check with your district technology personnel. Video files are large. Exporting video often takes at least as long as playing the video, if not longer. Making video files available for others in the class can also present challenges; due to their large size, video files do

not share well over email. Sharing files through cloud-based storage such as OneDrive or Google Drive can overcome these limitations.

Online Projects: Hyperdocs, Websites, Blogs, Wikis and Online Portfolios

What are they?
We grouped these projects together because they have similar characteristics. Each of these genres allows for the incorporation of text, image, video, and sound. All are displayed through a web browser to the consumer. In order to fully consider the creation of an online project, one must also explore the considerations for each type of media (print, video, image, sound) that is part of that project. One of the advantages of an online project is the ability to present information in a non-linear order, allowing for hypertext to link together any two pieces of information. Hyperdocs are digital documents where all materials (links, videos, charts, etc.) needed for the lesson or activity are included in the document, and are designed to have students engage in collaborative work. Similarly, classroom websites, blogs and wikis allow teachers and students to curate a space to celebrate books they are reading, pieces they are writing and thought-exchanges that honor the learning that is happening in the classroom.

Tools for Creating Online Projects
We do suggest that teachers check with their own district technology personnel before choosing a platform and provide this list as a starting point:

- Hyperdocs: Google Slides, Google Docs, Office Online
- Websites / Portfolios: Google Sites, Weebly, WordPress
- Blogs: Blogger, EduBlogs, Weebly, WordPress
- Wikis: PBWorks, Wikidot

Examples of Multimodal Learning Through Online Projects with YA Texts
Students need the chance to collaborate, to be creative, and to engage in experiences that support the ways in which they learn. When used effectively, multimodal learning experiences provide for all of these needs. The suggested texts below allow for multimodal investigative projects.

- ***Patron Saints of Nothing* by Randy Ribay (2019)**
  This novel takes readers to the Philippines where they grapple with the dehumanizing dictatorship of Rodrigo Duterte. This novel becomes a call to action; students are driven by the idea that Duterte is more than

a mere villainous character in a novel, but a violent political leader in reality.

- *Front Desk* **by Kelly Yang (2018)**
  In this middle-grade novel, the story follows the main character, Mia Tang, whose immigrant family works and lives in a motel and Mia herself manages the front desk. This novel gives students an opportunity to empathize and read through a lens where conversations around immigration can begin.
- *Radiant Child* **Javaka Steptoe (2016)**
  Engaging in multimodality while reading this biographical picture book allows students to see and discuss works by Jean-Michel Basquiat, a Puerto Rican-Haitian-American artist.

Considerations Specific to Online Projects

First and foremost, there should be a classroom, department, or grade-level site that is used to present the work students are doing. The teacher's role should shift to facilitator with students taking the reins and driving the content. Online projects can showcase students' writing and ideas from the novels read. These projects are best used when students are collaborating with one another. Collecting information on essential concepts, keeping a record of thoughts and reflections, posing questions to others, and designing storyboards highlight the versatility of hyperdocs, classroom websites, blogs and wikis.

Considerations for Educators

There are some general overarching considerations for engaging in multi-modal projects through technology. We choose the term considerations in lieu of best practices because what is "best" is highly dependent on the students using the technology and the available resources at the district and classroom levels.

Copyright

When incorporating stock images or audio clips, it is important to address copyright. Directly embedding copyrighted media in any of the projects we've mentioned is against the law in the United States, synonymous with copying and pasting text from a book onto a website. Creative Commons attempts to provide clearly labeled, free-to-use media. The creative commons licensing system allows for creators of work to specify the required terms in order to use their material for free. For more information on Creative Commons, see https://www.creativecommons.org.

Accessibility

When creating audiovisual projects, it is good practice to ensure that students are creating fully accessible projects, if possible. Accessibility principles state that everyone should be able to access an alternative form of media if needed. The most common accessibility features include captions for video, and alt text for screen readers. Free caption generators can be found online through a web search. Directions for adding both captions and alt text can be found in the help section of the specific software that is being used.

Digital Citizenship

When educators start talking about digital citizenship they place a lot of emphasis on cyber-safety. However, when looking at each component of digital citizenship, it is really asking educators to consider how they are teaching students to be active, productive, respectful citizens who contribute to a digital world in a positive way. These skills need to be taught; it isn't enough for students to have a basic understanding of what digital citizenship is. Students need multiple opportunities to apply these skills in real world contexts. Using multimodal approaches, students practice digital citizenship by advocating for change, engaging in respectful conversations with others who share different perspectives, and learning how to question the validity of online sources. Google Interland (https://beinternetawesome.withgoogle.com/en_us/interl and), Digital Citizenship from Common Sense (https://www.commonsense. org/education/digital-citizenship), and DigCitCommit (https://digcitcom mit.org/resources) are all great resources to start with.

Digital Equity

Teachers need to be cognizant of the digital divide that still exists among students, especially in K-12 settings. When assigning projects that are to be completed out of class, it is important to ensure that students have access to the technology and support to complete those projects.

Questions to ask include:

- Do all my students have high-speed internet?
- Can students bring equipment home to complete the project outside of class time?

- Do students understand how to problem solve their own technological issues?

If the answers to each of these questions are not a resounding "yes," then the teacher may benefit from devoting time in class to the most technologically demanding tasks.

Continuing to Grow Professionally

In order to stay current with effective instructional technology, teachers must value their own education. Looking at the role technology has played in the last decade, and the latest updates and tools that are created each year, it is important for teachers to continue furthering their pedagogy. ISTE (2020) Standards for Educators states that "educators continually improve their practice by learning from and with others and exploring proven and promising practices that leverage technology to improve student learning." The International Literacy Association (2017) has also placed importance on being an educator who is always learning by stating "Candidates demonstrate the ability to reflect on their professional practices, belong to professional organizations, and are critical consumers of research, policy, and practice" (p. 3). Subscribing to peer-reviewed journals of professional organizations, finding webinars, and attending conferences are ways to help keep up with advances in educational technology. And just like the teacher in the opening vignette, cultivating a Professional Learning Network (PLN) of other educators will allow classroom connections beyond local communities.

Conclusion

Multimodal learning opportunities facilitated through the use of instructional technology can engage students in work that supports all learners and connects them to the world. Starting with a foundational knowledge of what makes instructional technology implementation effective using TPACK and SAMR, and including activities that support multimodality, teachers and their students will have learning experiences that honor the stories and cultural connections found in global children's and YA literature. While planning for the effective use of technology and multimodal practices does take a lot of time, we argue that it is worth it to build the next generation of global citizens who demonstrate cultural competence and technological capability.

Discussion Questions

1. How can you implement multimodal approaches to enhance literacy based meaning making activities in your classroom?
2. How might using the TPACK and SAMR frameworks enhance your literacy instruction?

References

Boyd, F. B., & Tochelli, A. L. (2014). Multimodality and literacy learning. In K. A. Hinchman & H. K. Sheridan-Thomas (Eds.), *Best practices in adolescent literacy instruction* (2nd ed., pp. 291–307). The Guilford Press.
Cope, B., & Kalantzis, M. (2009). "Multiliteracies": New literacies, new learning. *Pedagogies, 4*(3), 164–195. https://doi.org/10.1080/15544800903076044
Dalton, B. (2012). Multimodal composition and the common core state standards. *The Reading Teacher, 66*(4), 333–339. https://doi.org/10.1002/TRTR.01129
Fisher, D., Frey, N., & Hattie, J. A. C. (2016). *Visible learning for literacy: Implementing the practices that work best to accelerate student learning: grades K-12*. Corwin.
International Literacy Association. (2017). *Standards for the preparation of literacy professionals 2017.* https://literacyworldwide.org/docs/default-source/resource-documents/draft-ila-standards-2017.pdf
International Society for Technology in Education (ISTE). (2020). *ISTE standards for educators.* https://www.iste.org/standards/for-educators
Jewitt, C. (2009). An introduction to multimodality. In *The Routledge handbook of multimodal analysis* (pp. 14–27). Routledge.
Koehler, M. J., & Mishra, P. (2009). What is technological pedagogical content knowledge? *Contemporary Issues in Technology and Teacher Education, 9*(1), 60–70.
Kress, G. R. (2003). *Literacy in the new media age*. Routledge.
Kress, G. R., & van Leeuwen, T. (2001). *Multimodal discourse: The modes and media of contemporary communication*. Oxford University Press.
McNair, J. C. (2016). #WeNeedMirrorsAndWindows: Diverse classroom libraries for K–6 Students. *The Reading Teacher, 70*(3), 375–381. doi: https://doi.org/10.1002/trtr.1516
Paris, D., & Alim, H. S. (2017). *Culturally sustaining pedagogies: Teaching and learning for justice in a changing world*. Teachers College Press.
Puentedura, R. R. (2015). *SAMR: A brief introduction* (pp. 1–12). https://hippasus.com/rrpweblog/archives/2015/10/SAMR_ABriefIntro.pdf
Routman, R. (2018). *Literacy essentials: Engagement, excellence, and equity for all learners*. Stenhouse Publishers.
Rowsell, J. (2013). *Working with multimodality: Rethinking literacy in a digital age*. Routledge.

Serafini, F., & Gee, E. (2017). *Remixing multiliteracies: Theory and practice from New London to new times.* Teachers College Press.

Takacs, Z. K., & Bus, A. G. (2018). How pictures in picture storybooks support young children's story comprehension: An eye-tracking experiment. *Journal of Experimental Child Psychology, 174,* 1–12. https://doi.org/10.1016/j.jecp.2018.04.013

Tavernicr, M. (2016). Exploring the suitability of the book creator for iPad app for early childhood education. In D. Churchill, J. Lu, T. K. F. Chiu, & B. Fox (Eds.), *Mobile learning design: Theories and application.* Springer Singapore. https://doi.org/10.1007/978-981-10-0027-0

Taylor, S. V., & Leung, C. B. (2020). Multimodal literacy and social interaction: Young children's literacy learning. *Early Childhood Education Journal, 48*(1), 1–10. https://doi.org/10.1007/s10643-019-00974-0

Books Cited

Colfer, E., Donkin, A., & Rigano, G. (2017). *Illegal: A graphic novel telling one boy's epic journey to Europe.* Hodder Children's Books.

Khorram, A. (2019). *Darius the Great is not okay.* Penguin Books.

Reynolds, J. (2020). *Stamped.* Little, Brown and Co.

Ribay, R. (2019). *Patron saints of nothing.* Penguin Books.

Sáenz, B. A. (2012). *Aristotle and Dante discover the secrets of the universe.* Simon & Schuster BFYR.

Steptoe, J. (2019). *Radiant child the story of young artist Jean-Michel Basquiat.* Findaway World, LLC.

Venkatraman, P. (2019). *The bridge home.* Puffin Books, an imprint of Penguin Random House LLC.

Yang, K. (2018). *Front desk.* Arthur Levine.

Contributors

Maria Acevedo-Aquino is an Associate Professor at Texas A&M San Antonio. Her research interests include Latinx children's literature, and play, inquiry, and story as transformative experiences in early childhood education.

Jennifer Ashton, Ph.D. (University of Rochester) is an Associate Professor in the Department of Education and Human Development at SUNY Brockport. She studies contemporary special education practice from a Disability Studies in Education perspective and has written several scholarly articles involving critical analysis of co-teaching.

Shelby Boehm is a doctoral student at the University of Florida and a former high school English teacher. She has been published in journals such as *English Leadership Quarterly, Journal of Media Literacy Education, and Study and Scrutiny: Research on Young Adult Literature.*

Kathleen Colantonio-Yurko, Ph.D., is an Assistant Professor of Literacy at SUNY Brockport where she teaches courses in secondary literacy education. Kathleen was a secondary ELA teacher for many years in Florida. She earned her PhD from the University of Florida.

Amanda Flugel, M.Ed. (SUNY Brockport) holds teaching certifications in Childhood 1-6 and Students with Disabilities 1-6 and has met requirements for certification in Literacy (B-12) and Early Childhood B-2. She is a recent graduate and is in the early stages of her teaching career.

Dori Harrison, Ph.D., is an Assistant Professor of Education at Ohio State University-Newark. Her research centers on language and literacy practices in education. She explores how educators understand and use multicultural and multilingual practices to create spaces of resistance or transformation for children.

Meredith Hutchings is an elementary school teacher, former graduate research assistant and a recent literacy MA graduate from SUNY Brockport. She holds a B.A. in Childhood Inclusive Education also from SUNY Brockport.

Gina Kelly is a school counselor in Port Washington, NY. She holds a B.A. in Psychology from Molloy College and a M.Ed in School Counseling from Queens College, CUNY. She is certified in School Building Leadership (SBL) and School District Leadership (SDL) from Stony Brook University.

Grace Kelly, M.Ed. (SUNY Brockport) holds teaching certifications in childhood and early childhood inclusive education, and literacy. Grace worked as the Assistant Director for SummerLEAP at SUNY Brockport. She was named one of National Afterschool Association's Next Generation of Afterschool Leaders 2021.

Patricia Paugh is an Associate Professor, University of Massachusetts Boston. Her research interests include critical and disciplinary literacies, urban school classroom research, and collaborative teacher inquiry. She has previously published three books in the field of literacy education.

Janeen Pizzo holds a MS.Ed. from Saint Bonaventure University and is New York State certified in English 7-12 and Literacy 5-12. She is an ISTE Certified Educator and is currently a Lecturer of Literacy in the Education and Human Development Department at SUNY Brockport.

Logan Rath holds a MLS from the University at Buffalo and MS in Information Design and Technology from SUNY Polytechnic. He recently completed his doctoral studies in education at the University at Buffalo and is working as an instruction librarian at SUNY Brockport where he supports education students.

Holly Spinelli teaches secondary English. She holds a M.A. in English from Bread Loaf School of English and a M.A.T. in English from New York University. Her awards include: Emmy Award contributing writer, Academy for Teachers Fellow, and the Alice Trillin Teaching Award.

Amy Shema, Ph.D. is a lecturer at SUNY Brockport in the Department of Education and Human Development. She works to establish meaningful collaborations with school and community partners. Her research interests include increasing family engagement and developing community and school partnerships.

Pamela Tirrito is a Reading Specialist in Port Washington, NY. She holds a B.A. in Elementary Education and a M.S. in Reading from Queens College, CUNY. She is certified in Reading Recovery from New York University.

Mario Worlds is a doctoral candidate in the College of Education at the University of Florida with a concentration in language and literacy instruction. He was recently awarded the Paul and Kate Farmer English Journal Writing Award in 2019. Currently, he teaches 7th grade reading.

Made in United States
North Haven, CT
15 August 2023